Cambridge Elements ≡

Elements in Contentious Politics
edited by
David S. Meyer
University of California, Irvine
Suzanne Staggenborg
University of Pittsburgh

THE ANARCHIST TURN IN TWENTY-FIRST CENTURY LEFTWING ACTIVISM

John Markoff
University of Pittsburgh

Hillary Lazar
University of Pittsburgh

Benjamin S. Case
Arizona State University

Daniel P. Burridge
The University of North Carolina

CAMBRIDGE
UNIVERSITY PRESS

Shaftesbury Road, Cambridge CB2 8EA, United Kingdom

One Liberty Plaza, 20th Floor, New York, NY 10006, USA

477 Williamstown Road, Port Melbourne, VIC 3207, Australia

314–321, 3rd Floor, Plot 3, Splendor Forum, Jasola District Centre, New Delhi – 110025, India

103 Penang Road, #05–06/07, Visioncrest Commercial, Singapore 238467

Cambridge University Press is part of Cambridge University Press & Assessment, a department of the University of Cambridge.

We share the University's mission to contribute to society through the pursuit of education, learning and research at the highest international levels of excellence.

www.cambridge.org
Information on this title: www.cambridge.org/9781009495240
DOI: 10.1017/9781009495219

When citing this work, please include a reference to the DOI 10.1017/9781009495219

First published 2024

A catalogue record for this publication is available from the British Library.

ISBN 978-1-009-49524-0 Hardback
ISBN 978-1-009-49522-6 Paperback
ISSN 2633-3570 (online)
ISSN 2633-3562 (print)

The Anarchist Turn in Twenty-First Century Leftwing Activism

Elements in Contentious Politics

DOI: 10.1017/9781009495219
First published online: March 2024

John Markoff
University of Pittsburgh

Hillary Lazar
University of Pittsburgh

Benjamin S. Case
Arizona State University

Daniel P. Burridge
The University of North Carolina

Author for correspondence: John Markoff, jm2@pitt.edu

Abstract: Leftwing activism of recent decades exhibits an anarchist turn evident in quantitative indicators like mentions of anarchists in news reports and by activists adopting anarchist modes of organization, tactics, and social goals – whether or not they claim that label. It is argued that the very crises that generated radical mobilizations since the turn of the millennium have led activists both to reject other strategies for social transformation and to see anarchist practices as appropriate to the challenges of our time. This turn is clearly apparent in the Americas and Europe, and has reverberations on an even broader transnational, perhaps global, scale. This suggests the need for research on social movements to more fully consider anarchists and other marginalized radical traditions, not just as objects of study but as important sources of theory.

Keywords: anarchism, social movements, revolution, democracy, globalization

ISBNs: 9781009495240 (HB), 9781009495226 (PB), 9781009495219 (OC)
ISSNs: 2633-3570 (online), 2633-3562 (print)

Contents

1 The Anarchist Turn in Word and Deed

In the opening decades of the twenty-first century, observers, including scholars, journalists, and activists, have been noting a shift in the ways leftwing movements orient toward power and hierarchy. With pleasure or concern, many onlookers are seeing a strong infusion of ideas and practices aligned with anarchism into major social movement mobilizations (Epstein 2001; Graeber 2002, 2008, 2013; Graeber and Grubačić 2004; Cornell 2011; Blumenfeld et al. 2013; Williams 2017, 2018; Dupuis-Déri 2019; Chase-Dunn and Almeida 2020; Manski et al. 2020).

We explore here the thesis of an *anarchist turn* in movement activism on the Left (Blumenfeld et al. 2013). While we argue that this is a transnational, perhaps global, phenomenon, following our experience and areas of study, our focus here is largely on the Americas, Europe, and the Levant. We present several kinds of empirical evidence, including big data, qualitative research, and a look at contemporary activism in various places that highlight how anarchists understand the current moment. The term "anarchism" is becoming more prominent compared with alternative leftwing ideological frameworks like "socialism," revealing growing attention to these theories and practices from proponents, adversaries, and observers alike. But the anarchist turn is not limited to terminology; as we will show, the activism of many who call themselves by other labels, or none at all, is increasingly imbued with anarchist practices.

What is a *turn*? Here, we describe it as the growing prevalence of practices, organizational forms, historical reference points, and discourse associated with anarchism. What is anarchism? There are no uncontroversial answers, but at its core, anarchism is about critiquing, dismantling, and proposing alternatives to formal power hierarchies. The word is derived from the Ancient Greek word, *an-arkhiā* (ἀναρχία), meaning *contrary to authorities, without a ruler,* or *against rule.* Anarchism has long been considered a brand of revolutionary socialism, breaking with other socialists and communists over anarchists' rejection of the state and critique of domination in any form.

Broadly speaking, for anarchists, the primary aims are ensuring freedom from top-down coercion and the ability for all people (and other living beings) to attain their highest possible self-actualization and well-being. And although there are some who embrace total individual autonomy, this typically implies a shared commitment to creation of deeply participatory and directly democratic societies. There also tends to be an emphasis on principles of voluntary association (the ability to choose with whom and how to associate); mutual aid (cooperation and reciprocity, which, for activists, is often fueled by a shared sense of struggle); antiauthoritarianism (with the state as the highest, though not the only, expression of top-down authority); decentralization and horizontality (to diffuse power); autonomy (and by extension self-governance); direct action (as a necessary method for achieving liberation); and prefigurative practice (putting revolutionary ideals into practice in the here and now, an important legacy of the New Left of the 1960s and 1970s [Breines 1989]) (Ward 1996; Graeber 2008, 2013; Grubačić & Graeber 2004; Kinna 2009, 2020; Marshall 2009; Gordon 2010; Shantz 2010; Hammond 2015; Williams 2017, 2018; Lazar 2018).

Analyzing anarchism and anarchists poses a challenge: anarchists are opposed to authorities, often including those conceptually imposed by hard definitions. In defining anarchist beliefs and practices, therefore, we use the following five characteristics, following Wittgenstein's notion of *family resemblance*, the idea that a group of things can be connected via overlapping similarities despite no single defining feature being necessarily common to all of them (Wittgenstein 2009: 67–77).

- Autonomy. Emphasis on uncoerced voluntary association in a participatory society. Decision-making at some level must be via agreement or *consensus*, as majority votes against fervent opposition from a minority are often considered a manifestation of violent domination, and coercing participation from anyone is anathema. This principle shows up in favored watchwords like *antiauthoritarian*, whether talking about states or interpersonal relations, and stresses both personal and collective freedom as well as transformative social relations that bring individuals' and communities' interests closer together.

- Egalitarianism. The anarchist conviction is that human relations should be evaluated along ethical dimensions, specifically a cooperative ethic, rather than instrumental and transactional ones. This is grounded in the underlying equality of all. Rather than liberalism's equality of rights alone, anarchists, like many others, prefer *equity*, meaning the redress of current inequalities as necessary on the way to a more egalitarian and emancipatory society. This, like the opposition to all forms of domination, also distinguishes anarchists from rightwing libertarians or "anarcho-capitalists," who oppose the state in favor of social Darwinism, individualism, and radical market economics. But the ethical dimension also distinguishes them from important currents in the history of socialism, which centered class interest as the root of all sociopolitical inequalities. Today's anarchists are likely to criticize multiple, interlocking axes of domination and socio-structural oppression.

- Horizontality. Organization comes through participatory democracy, for example, community groups, action teams, workers' councils, or rotating and recallable delegates to wider federations that govern via coordination rather than hierarchical, centralized command, or coercion. This means opposition to the democratic centralist organizational structure typically associated with Leninist movements, the elected representation of liberal democracy, the authoritarianism of the capitalist workplace, the tyranny of the hetero-patriarchal family, and state power itself. The state is seen as an instrument of coercion and violence, even when controlled by groups claiming to act on behalf of justice, equality, and freedom. Along with horizontalism comes an emphasis on *decentralization* – on local and often consensus-based decision-making structures. Individuals, organizations, and ad hoc action groups may seek out wider alliances of greater or less durability when deemed advantageous, but always with the autonomy to withdraw.

- Direct action. Anarchists oppose the state's totalizing authority, and capitalism's monetization imperative though direct action, meaning individuals and collectives moving directly to solve problems and meet needs. In its oppositional form, this can manifest through contentious public or covert actions that disrupt systems of domination, or though propaganda, vandalism, and street art. Direct action can also refer to taking personal and collective responsibility for the needs and well-being of others as part of collective struggle for a better world. One of its most prominent forms is *mutual aid*: the idea of cooperation, reciprocity, and support rather than competition for resources, paternalistic charity, or bureaucratic programs reliant on state coercion.

- Prefiguration. If there is a path to a better world, then the movements that fight for it promise to not only bring about that world in the future but also manifest it through their practices, organizational structure, and lived values through *praxis*. Movement organizations are not simply instruments for achieving the conquest of state power and then using that victory for social transformation. Rather, the movement itself is understood to be the locus of transformational change in the present. Among other things, this often manifests through skepticism about charismatic (typically male) leaders and diligent attention to combatting the replication of social, cultural, and gendered hierarchies within movement spaces. The prefigurative ethic is related to anti-utopianism; anarchists tend to reject the notion that utopia is achievable or desirable. The revolution is not an event but a process, and for anarchists, the prefigurative process is never-ending. There is no final struggle, rejecting an important idea in much of the history of revolutionary socialism.

The terms, beliefs, and dispositions just mentioned denote anarchist practices while acknowledging that many anarchists do not associate with all of them nor do they uniquely exist within anarchism, but a variety of currents that intersect, overlap, and resonate with one another. Many who do embrace these principles may not self-identify with anarchism. As scholars like Dana Williams (2017: 7–9) have pointed out, there is a conceptual stickiness to determining who or what explicitly constitutes an "anarchist." Spencer Sunshine notes that too often, practices associated with anarchism are lumped under that label without any conceptual distinctions (2013), while Spencer Potiker suggests the need to distinguish between "anarchist" and "anarchistic" (2019). Williams proposes a spectrum for thinking about who an anarchist is: explicitly anarchist (self-identifying individuals whose values and practices are aligned with anarchism), improperly anarchist (those who identify but whose practices are at odds with anarchist values), implicitly anarchist (those in line with anarchist values who do not identify with it), and non-anarchist. David Graeber and Andrej Grubačić (2004) distinguish between the older, more sectarian, and overtly anarchist organizing efforts that were an important part of western radicalism in the 1960s and 1970s, and a newly emergent and growing presence of "small-a" anarchists who tended to be younger, affiliated with transnational mobilizations and influenced by "indigenous, feminist, ecological and cultural-critical ideas" (2004). Indeed, whether "big" or "small a," today's anarchism draws on many, diverse radical traditions reflecting cross-pollination of movements; critical interventions, for example, by feminists and queer activists; and importantly, a shared goal of working toward an egalitarian, emancipatory society across many varied mobilizations (Lazar 2018).

Related to this latter point, we should also consider what could be called an "anarchist spirit," following Bamyeh (2010), or even simply a human impulse toward freedom that has existed throughout history (Scott 2009; Craib and Maxwell 2015; Ramnath 2019). Our goal is not to assign a label to anyone. It is to identify and explain a transformational phenomenon in recent decades, in which the organizational norms, behaviors, and languages of the Left, broadly defined, are becoming more decentralized, less hierarchical, concerned with undoing social power dynamics (including within movement organizations), and deploying terms, forms, and practices that are found in anarchist theories and histories.

We are building on these prior observations to argue that: (1) there is a substantial presence of expressly anarchist activists working with and alongside non-anarchists in today's transnational, national, and local movements; (2) there are many more who enact or espouse anarchist values without the self-identification, and that this number seems to be growing in many parts of the world. In other words, much of the turn we are looking at would largely fall under Williams' classification of "implicit anarchist" and Graeber and Grubačić's "small-a" anarchism.

This Element explores the anarchist turn in two parts, documenting the turn and then explaining it. In the first, we present quantitative data demonstrating that in the late twentieth and early twenty-first centuries, terms identifying people or actions with "anarchism" are on the rise in many places, especially striking relative to "socialism" – the other major radical current on the Left. Impressive as this shift has been, actions, organizations, or movements explicitly identified with anarchism are only part of the story. We also present evidence that anarchist models are being engaged by individual activists and organizations that do not self-identify with anarchism. Here we draw on secondary sources and interviews with US and Central American activists as well as broader analyses of contemporary movements. Again, we focus on the western hemisphere and Europe, and to a lesser extent, the Levant, where much of our experience and expertise is, although we make connections to other parts of the world, pointing to a global, albeit uneven and certainly not universal, phenomenon.

Second, we attempt an explanation. On the one hand, there remains a need for a radical Left challenge to the status quo. The fusion of capitalist economies and liberal democratic electoral systems has not delivered on most people's needs and aspirations, instead fueling inequality and failing political systems with rapidly eroding legitimacy. Meanwhile, increasingly evident climate collapse imparts an anxious urgency enhanced by the growing strength of powerful currents on the political Right (in part fueled by the same set of failures of capitalism and liberal democracy). On the other hand, the main leftwing alternatives to anarchism, state socialism and democratic socialism, lost a great deal of credibility with the collapse of the Soviet Union, the Chinese Communist Party turning to authoritarian capitalism, and European welfare states caving in to neoliberalism. Electorally competitive Socialist parties sometimes brought important reforms but never transcended capitalism, even when this was an avowed goal (as it was in Europe a century ago). The anarchist position was validated by these developments, having levied critiques against its Left cousins all along that anticipated and explained their deteriorations. Furthermore, anarchists' visions of a better world increasingly speak to the compounding problems of our global age and the intertwining of struggles against domination, including on bases of race, class, gender, sexuality, citizenship, and all ways in which people are exploited and oppressed, within a coherent theory of power; willingness to directly confront forces of the Far Right; rethinking what democracy should mean and how to build a more participatory society; and uncompromising opposition to a society based on profit, privilege, extraction, and control, instead proposing an ethics of free cooperation, solidarity, and regeneration.

In making this argument, it is not our intention to litigate the old anarchism-versus-Marxism debate, or to make claims about the state's role in revolutionary struggle. Our personal sympathies notwithstanding, the argument here is a *descriptive* one; we are observing and providing evidence for a significant shift toward anarchist modes of organizing, both explicit and implicit, in many places around the world. Our goal in explicating the anarchist turn is to improve the understanding of social movement mobilizations in our time.

2 Counting Anarchism

2.1 Sifting Through a Lot of Words

We use Google's Ngram Viewer to explore change over time in the relative prominence of anarchist and socialist labels. This tool allows one to examine the frequency of word use in a vast corpus of 8 million digitized books, as of 2011, with a half trillion words in eight languages, a subset of 15 million books mostly from university library collections (Michel et al. 2011: 176; Pechenick et al. 2015: 1). The dataset has since expanded. In this Element, we focus on the ratio of the occurrence of "anarchism" to "socialism," "anarchists" to "socialists," and "anarchist" to "socialist" as well as corresponding terms[1] in the other languages in the Google corpus.

Anyone who has spent even a little time considering the vast literature on these two political categories will see the difficulties in doing this. Both terms have complex and overlapping histories, with contradictory practices claiming their mantles. Their histories have also been deeply intertwined, and some practices today that we will refer to as anarchist were considered socialism in the middle of the nineteenth century. We write in awareness that, like "democracy," "socialism," and "anarchism" have always been deeply contested (Gallie 1956) – and that not all of today's activists have interest in distinguishing these terms. Nevertheless, comparing the levels of usage of these two terms gives us purchase on their comparative salience for different generations of movements

---

[1] By "corresponding term," we mean the ideological label (anarchism, *Anarchismus*, *anarchisme*, and so on), the plural label for activists (anarchists, *Anarchisten*, *anarchistes*, and so on), and the adjectival form (anarchist, *anarchistisch*, *anarchiste*, and so on). As in all translations, the correspondences are imperfect. In English, for example, anarchist is both an adjective and a singular noun; in Spanish, the relevant people are often "libertarios"; in Russian, both nouns and adjectives are declined and take case endings. (We only present graphs for the Russian nominative forms but have verified that the analysis is unaltered if the other forms are counted, and have similarly checked for declined adjectives in German.)

as well as the scholars analyzing them and the governments attempting to repress them.

There are additional important cautions. Books are not all that is printed and may represent even less well what is spoken; the Google collection is but a subset of all books (one estimate makes it about 4 percent of all published books [Nunberg 2010: 1]); the smaller, though still vast, subset used by the Ngram Viewer may not be representative of the full corpora; the optical character recognition may make errors (some comical – see Zhang 2015); there are errors (sometimes large) in the dates given for texts; before 1800 counts rest on small numbers of books; books of vast cultural significance and those no one reads are equally weighty; and the Chinese materials present special problems (Google N-Grams and Pre-Modern Chinese 2015). Our choice of languages was dictated by the available datasets. The corpora vary in size: as of 2011, the English corpus was 361 billion words, the French and Spanish each 45 billion, German 37 billion, Russian 31 billion, Chinese 13 billion, and Hebrew a comparatively modest 2 billion (Michel et al. 2011: 176). There are languages spoken by more than 100 million people, not among those included by Google (e.g., Arabic and Hindi), as well as many others spoken by fewer.

So one would not want to rely on the Ngrams alone. But we do get a sense of what people were writing in eight languages and therefore what was out there for readers of those languages to read.[2]

Let us start with English, which has some recent claim to be a global language (Northrup 2013). Figure 1a presents the occurrence of the terms "anarchist," "anarchists," and "anarchism" – that is, the adjectival qualifier, the activists, and the ideology – within the millions of books in English over time. We start from the 1880s because that is when these terms began to be used with increasing frequency and end in 2019 because that is when the publicly accessible data ends. There was a significant ascent in the 1960s, peaking in 1972, followed by a decline that did not, however, fall back to the levels of the 1940s and 1950s. But from the late 1980s, there is a steep ascent, attaining heights never seen before by the second decade of the twenty-first century.

What we will mean by an anarchist turn, then, will be a rising presence of anarchist labels relative to those denoting other radical visions, organizations, and practices, in particular, socialism. Instead of comparing the frequencies over time of anarchist labels with all words, we will compare them to socialist labels, which have their own trajectory.[3] What of socialism? Figure 1b shows

---

[2] For other cautions about Ngram analysis, see Younes and Reips (2019), Zhang (2015), and "Should We Allow" (2012).

[3] This has the collateral virtue of mitigating one of the challenges to interpreting Ngram graphs through time: words are continuing to be created or forgotten (Michel et al. 2011) and changing

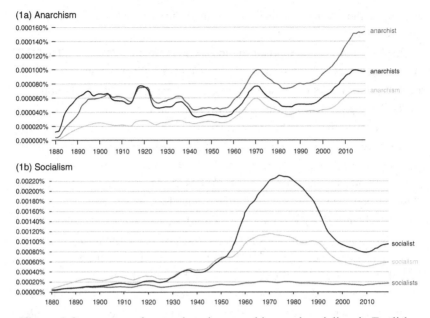

Figure 1 Occurrence of terms denoting anarchism and socialism in English, 1880–2019. Occurrence in books (%) by year.

Source: Google online Ngram Viewer (smoothing = 3) (https://books.google.com/ngrams)

that, for English, "socialist" falls off from its early-1970s peak until a modest comeback after 2010.[4]

Following the useful terminology of Robert Putnam's (2020: 169) use of Ngrams to chart US cultural change, we speak of the "cultural salience" of anarchism and socialism in eight languages. Noting that the Y-axes in Figure 1 show the proportion of the three words, both anarchist and socialist, among all English words, we see that there is no point at which anarchist terms are more numerous. If an anarchist turn means that it predominates, this has not happened. But Figure 1 leaves open the possibility that there may have been a strong shift in that direction.

Figures 2a through 2g graph the ratios over the years of anarchist terms to socialist ones in English, French, German, Spanish, Italian, Russian, and Hebrew (we will separately consider Chinese in Figure 2h). For these seven

---

numbers of books published on subjects unrelated to radical activism, raising problems in interpreting the sheer proportion of all words appearing in books, but except in Figure 1, we compare the frequency of anarchism to socialism, rather than to all words.

[4] Some readers of an earlier draft wondered whether we should have considered a larger set of radical identities, not just socialism, as alternatives to anarchism. Graphs comparing anarchism to the sum of socialism, Marxism, and communism for the seven languages in which we see an anarchist turn show that same turn. We only present the graphs for the most generic of these terms, socialism.

languages, there was a late-nineteenth-century high-relative salience of anarchism, for some languages extending into the early twentieth century, particularly in Russian and Hebrew up until the Russian Revolution of 1917. However, only for German, Russian, and Hebrew do anarchist terms ever outnumber socialist ones and only for the last of these does this happen in the twenty-first century.

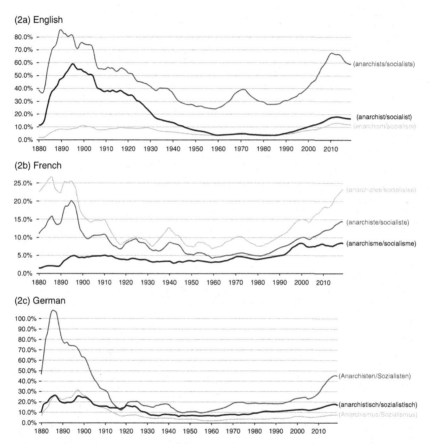

Figures 2 Ratios of frequencies of terms denoting anarchism to terms denoting socialism, 1880–2019, various languages, by year. (a) English, (b) French, (c) German, (d) Spanish, (e) Italian, (f) Russian, (g) Hebrew, (h) Chinese.

Note: Russian – анархисты/социалисты = anarchists/socialists; анархизм/социализм = anarchism/socialism; анархический+анархическій/социалистический = anarchist (adj.)/socialist (adj.). Anarchist (adj.) counts include the pre-1917 as well as the modern spelling.

Note: Hebrew – אנרכיסטים/סוציאליסטים = anarchists/socialists;אנרכיזם/סוציאליזם = anarchism/socialism; אנרכיסטי/סוציאליסטי = anarchist (adj.)/socialist (adj.).

Note: Chinese – 无政府主义者/社会主义者 = anarchists/socialists; 无政府主义/社会主义 = anarchism/socialism.

Source: Google online Ngram Viewer (smoothing = 3) (https://books.google.com/ngrams).

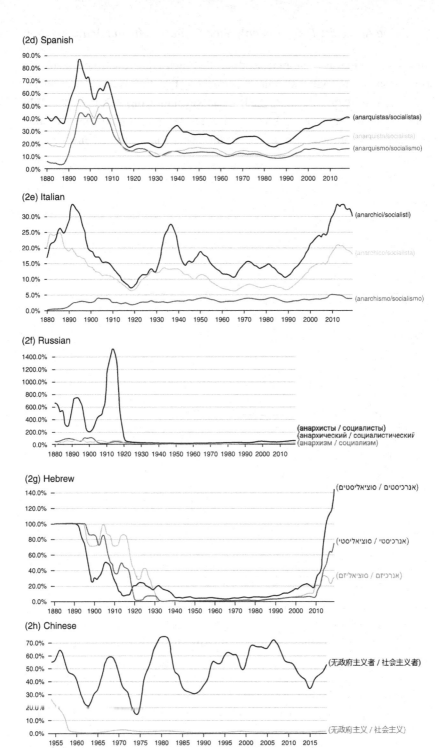

Figures 2 (cont.)

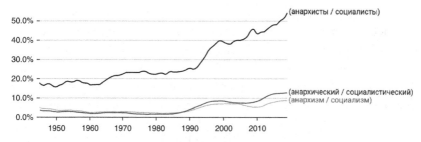

Figure 3 Ratios of frequencies of terms denoting anarchism to terms denoting socialism, 1945–2019, Russian, by year.

Note: анархисты/социалисты = anarchists/socialists; анархизм/социализм = anarchism/socialism; анархический/социалистический = anarchist (adj.)/socialist (adj)

Source: Google online Ngram Viewer (smoothing = 3) (https://books.google.com/ngrams)

But the figures also show that for all seven languages, there was a late twentieth- and early twenty-first-century relative rise. Since the large early peak makes this late twentieth-century trend especially hard to see in the Russian graph, we supplement Figure 2f with Figure 3 for Russian commencing with the end of the Second World War.

Overall, we see some interesting differences by language. The relative cultural salience of anarchism rises in English and French in the 1960s and a bit beyond and then declines before resuming a late twentieth-century ascent. In Spanish and Italian, it is a bit later when the post-1960's descent occurs and in German it never happens, but in all three, there is an ascent toward the end of the century. The increasing salience of anarchism from the 1960s on in Russian is broadly similar to the other languages, and it steeply accelerates from the breakup of the Soviet Union at the end of 1991. If we can take this to mean that something was happening in Russian in the last decades of the Soviet Union that resembled what was happening in French, German, or Italian, we can also turn this around and wonder if the end of the Soviet Union marked a cultural shift beyond the Soviet Union as well.

There are some differences in the patterns in the twenty-first century's second decade. English and Italian show a falloff, that is, a lessening of the relative salience of anarchism. In both, however, levels remained well above the 1990s. Spanish may have crested, and French, Russian,[5] and Hebrew show a continuing ascent. But in all seven languages, since the 1980s or 1990s, there has been a relative turn to people, or things, being designated with anarchist labels by the turn of the twenty-first century. Here is our anarchist turn.

---

[5] See Figure 3.

Finally, we comment on the Chinese data, displayed in Figure 2h. For books in Simplified Chinese that appear in the Google corpus, beginning with 1954 when this modification of printed Chinese was introduced, there is a continual seesaw in the cultural salience data.[6] The broad trends seen in the seven other languages do not appear. So, the anarchist turn in vocabulary shows up in languages read by a broad and varied, though bounded, part of humanity.[7]

2.2 Anarchists in the News

Table 1 compares mentions of anarchists, anarchism, and anarchist phenomena to socialists, socialism, and socialist phenomena in *The New York Times* by decade, with their ratio shown in Column 3.[8] Mentions of anarchism are fewer than mentions of socialism in every decade. As with the Ngram studies, if anarchist turn were to mean that explicit anarchist presence in the print media is greater than the socialist, that has not happened. Yet note that the ratio is the highest in the last two decades of the nineteenth century and then falls in the twentieth reaching its low point in the 1950s, after which it slowly rises for the rest of the century and then rises more rapidly in the twenty first.[9] Biases in newspaper coverage of protest have been known to social movement scholars for decades and remain a significant source of caution in the use of newspaper-derived data (e.g., Franzosi 1987; Davenport 2010). Nonetheless, we note the general convergence with the Ngram graphs (other than for Chinese) on an anarchist turn as we define it. Table 2 is a replication for the *Times of London* and Table 3 for the *Times of India*.[10] The London *Times* has a quite similar pattern. For the Indian *Times*, there may also be a small early twenty-first century anarchist turn, but it is much less pronounced. So leading newspapers aiming at global coverage, and which are based in current and previous globally hegemonic powers, show an anarchist turn and the leading paper of the largest postcolonial state may do so to a very modest degree as well.

---

[6] We thank Hanning Wang for advising us on the Chinese materials.

[7] The languages covered, numerous as their speakers are, are known to only a minority of the world population, although a substantial one. Data published by *Ethnologue* (2022) show that about 15% of the world population has one of the seven languages showing the anarchist turn as their first language. An even larger number has one as a second language (19%), especially English with its total 1.452 billion speakers worldwide. Somewhat over half the world's population speaks none of the eight included languages.

[8] We omit the 1850s and 1860s, when both terms were rare.

[9] At the point we consulted it, Proquest's historical database for the *New York Times* stopped in 2015. If we substitute Proquest's Recent Newspaper series, we get the marginally lower anarchism/socialism ratio of 0.21 for 2010–2019.

[10] There are some differences in the years covered and the search functions when we accessed the three databases.

Table 1 Terms referring to anarchism and socialism, *New York Times*,
1870–2015, by decade.

Decade	Anarchism[1] (a)	Socialism[1] (b)	Ratio (a/b)
1870–1879	21	771	0.03
1880–1889	1,363	2,120	0.64
1890–1899	2,573	3,869	0.67
1900–1909	2,193	5,365	0.41
1910–1919	2,016	11,833	0.17
1920–1929	1,287	14,894	0.09
1930–1939	1,169	29,808	0.04
1940–1949	349	21,921	0.02
1950–1959	268	27,373	0.01
1960–1969	730	22,742	0.03
1970–1979	979	23,122	0.04
1980–1989	808	19,350	0.04
1990–1999	750	10,057	0.07
2000–2009	817	4,280	0.19
2010–2015[2]	650	2,855	0.23
All years	*15,973*	*200,360*	*0.08*

Source: ProQuest *Historical Newspapers. The New York Times with Index.*
[1] ProQuest search terms used are anarchis[*2] and socialis[*2], which pick up the stem and
  two additional characters, that is, anarchism/anarchist/anarchists and socialism/socialist/
  socialists, capturing the movement label, the adjectival form, and the plural noun for
  activists.
[2] Incomplete decade.

2.3 Anarchists Writing for Anarchists

Williams and Lee (2012) and Williams (2017) have drawn on an anarchist project
to explore the multicountry vigor of the late twentieth-century and the early
twenty-first-century anarchism. Since 1995, the A-Infos website has been posting
brief news of anarchist activities to inform anarchists around the world.[11] By
2008, it had gathered "over sixty-thousand news items in over a dozen languages"
(Williams and Lee 2012: 7). Important for our arguments, it is "a multi-lingual
news service, by, for and about anarchists." One might wonder about both the
newspaper and Ngram data presented in earlier sections "Sifting through a lot of
words" and "Anarchists in the news" whether the use of "anarchism" and related
terms reflects to some degree either inaccurate attributions or malicious ones, but

---

[11] www.ainfos.ca/.

Table 2 Terms referring to anarchism and socialism, *Times of London*, 1870–2014, by decade.

Decade	Anarchism[1] (a)	Socialism[1] (b)	Ratio (a/b)
1870–1879	46	810	0.06
1880–1889	782	1,955	0.40
1890–1899	1,765	3,944	0.45
1900–1909	974	5,811	0.17
1910–1919	836	7,659	0.11
1920–1929	372	11,424	0.03
1930–1939	455	12,597	0.04
1940–1949	152	5,068	0.03
1950–1959	84	8,802	0.01
1960–1969	73	9,208	0.01
1970–1979	692	11,859	0.06
1980–1989	1,075	11,458	0.09
1990–1999	647	7,355	0.09
2000–2009	1,053	5,444	0.19
2010–2015[2]	352	2,375	0.15
All years	*9,358*	*105,769*	*0.09*

Source: *Times of London Digital Archive.*
[1] Search terms used are anarchists and socialists.
[2] Incomplete decade.

the writers and compilers of the A-Infos items were both knowledgeable and sympathetic. While we have found it difficult to use this source to study change over time, the enormous numbers of postings and their great geographic range add to the case for the vibrancy of contemporary anarchism. In the single week beginning November 8, 2022, for example, we found 177 posts. On November 11, to be even more specific, there were posts in English, French, Turkish, German, Italian, Portuguese, and Spanish and news about events in Poland, France, the USA, Italy, Denmark, Russia, Spain, Belarus, Argentina, and Chile. In addition to the languages just mentioned, A-Infos has posts in Greek, Chinese, Catalan, Dutch, Polish, Russian, Finnish, and Swedish. In another work, Williams and Lee (2008) study a multicountry listing of anarchist organizations, the Anarchist Yellow Pages – again compiled by anarchists for anarchists – and find 2,171 organizations listed in 2005, up by "over 40%" since 1997 (Williams and Lee 2008: 64). In the Anarchist Yellow Pages for 2005, there were twenty-one countries with at least twenty organizations. The uneven geographic coverage (especially large numbers in the wealthy democratic states) raises the possibility

Table 3 Terms referring to anarchism and socialism, *Times of India*, 1870–2009, by decade.

Decade	Anarchism[1] (a)	Socialism[1] (b)	Ratio (a/b)
1870–1879	3	129	0.02
1880–1889	80	379	0.21
1890–1899	318	580	0.55
1900–1909	727	1,483	0.49
1910–1919	874	3,124	0.28
1920–1929	365	2,774	0.13
1930–1939	282	5,004	0.06
1940–1949	41	4,007	0.01
1950–1959	56	15,613	0.00
1960–1969	89	11,043	0.01
1970–1979	141	11,513	0.01
1980–1989	92	6,758	0.01
1990–1999	113	5,433	0.02
2000–2009	107	2,307	0.05
All years	*3,268*	*70,147*	*0.05*

Source: ProQuest *Historical Newspapers. The Times of India.*
[1] ProQuest search terms used are anarchis[*2] and socialis[*2], which pick up the stem and two additional characters, that is, anarchism/anarchist/anarchists and socialism/socialist/socialists, capturing the movement label, the adjectival form, and the plural noun for activists.
[2] Incomplete decade.

that in places where it is not safe to announce oneself or with less access to internet and digital communications, there are undocumented organizations.[12]

2.4 A Survey of Activists

In counterpoint to the World Economic Forum of the managerial institutions of global capitalism, the World Social Forum was initiated in 2001 as a launching pad for a renewed global activism. Christopher Chase-Dunn and collaborators of the Transnational Social Movement Research Working Group at the University of California (Riverside) surveyed participants at the World Social Forum in Porto Alegre in 2005 and Nairobi in 2007, as well as participants in the US Social Forum in Atlanta 2007 and Detroit 2010, on their political identities

---

[12] In 2022, a US-based anarchist news site, *It's Going Down*, reported on fourteen countries, including Indonesia, Sudan, South Africa, and Chile (https://itsgoingdown.org/author/igd-worldwide).

and involvement in a wide variety of global issues. Although they only found a small number identifying as anarchists (ranging from 6 percent to 26 percent depending on which forum and which year), "anarchist activists are significantly younger than other activists and the whole sample of attendees" (Chase-Dunn et al. 2019: 380), indicating a generational shift. Of the 18- to 25-year-olds actively involved with some movement, 53 percent identified as anarchists, and 30 percent of those between the ages of 26 and 35 did as well. In addition, anarchists were reported to be engaged with all "movement themes" listed in the survey, including LGBTQ, Indigenous, Anti-racism, Feminism, Peace, Housing, Communism, and Socialism. Whatever the specific issue engaging the early twenty-first century transnational activists surveyed – including Communism and Socialism – there were anarchists among them.

Even more striking was the much larger presence of anarchist forms of organization – avoidance of formal hierarchy ("horizontalism"), consensus decision-making, distrust of states, and commitments to both personal freedom and social equality. An overall minority identified as anarchists, but a majority was drawing on what Chase-Dunn calls an "anarchist playbook" (Chase-Dunn et al. 2019: 377).

2.5 What the Numbers Tell Us

First, in most of the languages that can be surveyed by Ngram analysis, the cultural salience of anarchism relative to socialism was clearly ascending in the later twentieth century and continuing into the twenty-first. This holds for English, French, Spanish, Italian, German, Russian, and Hebrew, though not for Chinese, showing that a geographically diverse collection of human beings was reading books with a growing anarchist presence, relative to other radicalisms, though not everywhere.

Second, in newspaper reporting from the previous and current global hegemons, *The New York Times* and the *Times of London*, people, actions, and ideas characterized as anarchist were increasingly notable compared to people, actions, and ideas characterized as socialist. This is true of the *Times of India*, too, albeit much less so.

Third, sources in which anarchist organizations and individuals are writing for other anarchists show that significant mobilizations exist in an impressive number of countries, that such activities are increasing in the early twenty-first century, and that anarchists are communicating in many languages.

Fourth, a survey of transnationally oriented activists shows a small but notable presence of those identifying as anarchists, especially among the younger ones. But it also shows an extensive adoption of practices historically linked to anarchism (Chase-Dunn et al. 2019). This fourth finding is a bridge into our next and more extensive section on the anarchist presence among activists on the Left. Notable as the presence of people labeled by themselves or others as anarchists in the early twenty-first century, even more striking is the degree to which recent activists have been embracing anarchist-style politics and techniques, often without that label.

3 Anarchist Practice beyond "Anarchists"

In the previous section, we discussed quantitative evidence for an increased cultural salience of anarchism via the use of the word, but this hardly begins to cover the far-reaching adoption of anarchist practices by activists, including visions of a better future, strategies to advance toward those imagined futures, and the organizational vehicles for realizing those strategies.

3.1 The Anarchist Playbook in Twenty-First-Century Movements

As if acknowledging a new millennium with its shift away from some Left traditions, in 2000, after three quarters of a century, the historic Italian Communist Party newspaper, *L'Umanità*, founded by Antonio Gramsci, closed down. In its last years, the Party, renamed the Party of the Democratic Left, lost its prized role in governing Red Bologna, long a model Left municipality. Faced with loss of readers, its newspaper called it quits (Eley 2002: 491). A decade later, a featured article in the *International Socialist Review* admitted that "the broad ideas of anarchism have defined the political landscape" for contemporary social movements (Kerl 2010). The following year, the Occupy Wall Street rebellion exploded across the USA and beyond, itself following historic uprisings in Tunisia, Egypt, Greece, and Spain, changing both political conversations about inequality and the norms for subsequent social movement mobilizations.

Well beyond the movements of the early twenty-first century that call themselves anarchist, many exhibit anarchist traits like horizontality, mutual aid, emphasis on autonomy, and prefigurative practices.[13] In the following sections we present a far-from-exhaustive list of examples of anarchist practices in groups, formations, uprisings, and movements in which participants may not identify as anarchists.

3.2 The Zapatistas of Chiapas

Contemporary anarchism has drawn from many radical currents, from indigenous resistance against colonialism to early twentieth-century militant anti-capitalist

---

[13] For an excellent discussion of tactical diffusion of anarchism into other mobilizations from antinuclear to the Global Justice and anti-fascism, see Williams 2018.

trade unionism to the countercultural communes of the 1960s and the rebellious antiauthoritarianism of 1980s punk (Davies 1997). Many of the practices and tactical repertoires of the anarchist turn were informed by the Quaker- and feminist-led movements of the 1970s and 1980s (Epstein 1991; Cornell 2011, 2016). And it also reflects a strong theoretical resonance with Black feminism, queer theory, and social ecology among others (Dixon 2014; Lazar 2018). But let us start our account of recent anarchist practice with the catalytic role of the Zapatista uprising of 1994 in Chiapas, Mexico.

After more than a decade of inaction on land reform by Mexican authorities, on New Year's Day in 1994, the *Ejército Zapatista de Liberación Nacional* (Zapatista Army of National Liberation), a movement of indigenous men and women occupied seven towns in Chiapas to protest the impending North American Free Trade Agreement. Facilitated by new digital technologies (Bob 2005), word quickly spread of the Zapatistas' rebellion, proclaimed secession from the Mexican State, and establishment of autonomous communities. In so doing, this reignited a revolutionary sense of hope among the Left – yes, it *was* possible to challenge globalized neoliberal capitalism – helping to spark the Global Justice Movement (GJM, referred to by some activists as the alter-globalization movement) and infuse a new anarchist sensibility into the mobilizations at the millennium (Kingsnorth 2003; Callahan 2004; Reitan 2007; Klein 2015; Grubačić and O'Hearn 2016; Manski et al. 2020).

Zapatismo is historically significant in the anarchist turn but is also an excellent example of the complexity of discussing what constitutes anarchism. Although the Zapatistas are not themselves anarchists by label, *Zapatismo* is widely seen among the radical Left as a kind of anarchism in practice – or at least as anarchist-resonant (Grubačić and O'Hearn 2016). The autonomous communities not only repudiated rule by the Mexican state but embraced horizontal decision-making across communities through "*encuentros*" or "convergences." Leadership rotated within the revolutionary juntas that ran the communes, there was an emphasis on gender equality and equitable social relations, and they rejected rigid dogmas for emergent knowledge, expressed in their saying: "in walking we ask" (Klein 2015). These practices were deeply influential in the organizational structure of the GJM, imbuing it with an anarchist orientation (Kingsnorth 2003; Martínez and García 2004).

3.3 The Global Justice Movement

The transnational impact of the Zapatista revolt was immediately evident in the creation of People's Global Action (PGA), launched by the European delegates to the initial Zapatista *encuentro* in 1996. People's Global Action was instrumental in organizing the second *encuentro* in Spain the following year as well as the earliest mobilizations of the GJM such as Global Action Days, protesting the WTO in Geneva in May 1998, Carnival Against Capital in June 1999, as well as being one of the many players in the anti-WTO protests in Seattle later that year (Wood 2020, 2012; Graeber 2008; Juris 2008). No doubt the Marxist autonomous tradition in parts of Europe, which shares ideological terrain with the anti-statism of anarchism, helped to deepen the rapid spread and general receptivity to *Zapatismo* across European activist spheres (Katsiaficas 2006; Graeber 2008).

The "Battle of Seattle" – the fierce demonstrations against the WTO meeting in Seattle in November 1999 – was a tipping point both for the developing GJM and the popularization of anarchism in the Global North. Over several days, more than fifty thousand protesters from an expansive range of social justice movements took the streets, from revolutionary environmental groups to major unions and transnational NGOs (Manski et al. 2020).[14] As momentum grew over the course of the week, gaining numbers in the face of widespread police brutality, the "Seattle moment" marked a watershed in the struggle against global capitalism. Moreover, in terms of the turn toward anarchism, it not only represented one of the largest visible moments of self-identified anarchists but also helped to radicalize a new generation steeped in anarchist principles. And although the "black bloc" anarchist contingent garnered the most media attention, largely negative, for their willingness to destroy private property and directly confront authorities, Seattle also demonstrated to many the potency of an anarchist-influenced, anti-corporate uprising through organization and tactics rooted in direct democracy, horizontality, and prefigurative logics (Wood 2020; Maeckelberg 2011; Manski et al. 2020).

Less than a year after Seattle, European activists of varied political perspectives, including anarchists and others adopting anarchist practices, came together to disrupt meetings of the institutions of global finance in Prague, in "a key turning point, helping to strengthen and expand emerging anti-globalization activist networks in Europe and other parts of the world" (Juris 2008: 52). Anarchists were among the initial planners of the mobilization. In the planning, "decisions were made by consensus, and a 'spokescouncil' model was employed based on decentralized coordination among autonomous affinity groups" (Juris 2008: 127). The Prague protestors divided the city into zones so that differing tactical repertoires could coexist without having to agree on standardized routines for all, inspiring anti-corporate protestors all over Europe.

---

[14] The many sites of protest throughout Seattle that week make estimates of total numbers particularly uncertain, with some as high as 100,000.

Juris (2008: 127–155) identifies 35 major protests against corporate globalization from 1999 to 2007, detailing what each added to protestors' repertoires and the degree to which these events promoted transnational cross-pollination of these movements.[15] Chase-Dunn and Almeida (2020: 72–86) provide further compelling quantitative analyses of the extent of transnational activist learning from prior events and benefitting from previously developed organizational experience. As they describe the wide range of groups participating and learning from each other: "youth, leftist and green political party militants, labor unions, environmentalists, LGBTQ groups, indigenous peoples, feminists, anarchists, among many others."

As transnational activists who had participated in the *encuentros* went on to build the emergent alter-globalization movement evident in Seattle and European convenings, the confluence of Zapatismo with preexisting anarchist tendencies and traditions across the Global North resulted in a decentralized, horizontal, anti-systemic, transnational mobilization dedicated to challenging global capitalism and ushering in less corruptible forms of "real" direct democracy (Graeber 2008; Maeckelberg 2011, 2012).

Significantly, beyond simply mirroring the horizontal structure of the *encuentros*, these convenings also reflected other anarchist principles, including experimental, prefigurative "villages," which offered lodging, trainings, and a place for activists to connect (Prokosch and Raymond 2002; Juris 2012; Wood 2004, 2021; Reitan 2007). Many of the participants also self-organized into "affinity groups," borrowing from the anarchist past, specifically in early twentieth-century Spain, and then widely practiced in the US radicalism of the 1960s and 1970s.

Certainly, not all participants involved in the GJM identified as anarchists; but, as Barbara Epstein (2001) observes, the young anti-globalization activists had a marked "anarchist sensibility" reflected in their commitment to decentralization, direct democracy, egalitarianism, anti-capitalism, suspicion of the state, and "living according to one's values." She summarizes: "For them, anarchism is important mainly as an organizational structure and as a commitment to egalitarianism. It is a form of politics that revolves around the exposure of the truth rather than strategy. It is a politics decidedly in the moment" (Epstein 2001).

A long-time anarchist organizer who cut his political teeth during the Seattle protests recounts that prior to the WTO demonstrations, he was not terribly political or interested in labels; he was there to save the sea turtles. Once there,

---

[15] These protests took place in England, Germany, the USA, the Czech Republic, France, Brazil, Canada, Sweden, Spain, Italy, Ecuador, India, Switzerland, Mexico, Scotland, Mali, Venezuela, Pakistan, Greece, Russia, and Kenya.

however, he felt an affinity for those calling themselves anarchists and the "organizing principles," he saw in action: "horizontalism, egalitarianism, anti-hierarchy, anti-state, anti-capitalism, anti-police, solidarity ... the large tendenc[ies] within that movement."[16] Or, as Graeber put it in his reflections at the time, "Anarchism is the heart of the movement, its soul" (2002).

3.4 The 2011 Cycle of Contention

Although the focus of the mobilizations shifted to an anti-war effort after the US invasion of Iraq in 2003, the anarchist underpinnings were carried forward into the next major cycle of contention in 2011. Throughout that first decade of the 2000s, anarchist ideas continued to grow in prominence as the new social movement norm (Epstein 2001; Graeber 2002; Graeber and Grubačić 2004; Gordon 2010; Maeckelbergh 2012; Dixon 2014). As Uri Gordon noted in 2010: "The past ten years have seen the full-blown revival of a global anarchist movement, possessing a coherent core political practice, on a scale and scope of activity unseen since the 1930s," supplanting Marxism "as the chief point of reference for radical politics in advanced capitalist countries" (Gordon 2010: 414). Anarchism in this context is best understood as "primarily a political culture shared across a decentralized global network of affinity groups and collectives" (Gordon 2010: 415). And within this culture, there are common, identifiable characteristics such as direct-action and mutual aid techniques, horizontal organizing models, and a language rooted in traditional anarchism.

Anarchist practices were a key aspect of the so-called "Arab Spring" uprisings, the Spanish and Greek anti-austerity movements, the global Occupy movement, and the other mobilizations of 2011 (Castañeda 2012; Juris 2012; Milkman et al. 2012; Flesher Fominaya 2020). Each of these mobilizations reflected particular national concerns and contexts, but, like the alter-globalization movement, they were also responding to economic and social inequalities brought on by neoliberal global policies, corporate favoritism, and discontent with both authoritarian and nominally democratic systems of governance (Castañeda 2012; Halvorsen 2012; della Porta et al. 2017).

Mohammed Bamyeh (in Milkman et al. 2012: 16–18) writes of a new "global culture of protest" broadly shared among the mobilizations of 2011 that are consistent with anarchism, including a suspicion of parties and electoral politics; a rejection of Margaret Thatcher's "There Is No Alternative" mantra for neoliberal capitalism; an emphasis on a horizontal notion of "the people" as opposed to governing systems or major parties; the hope to give voice to the previously

---

[16] Unpublished interview in Pittsburgh by Hillary Lazar, May 2017.

voiceless; and an intentional vagueness around specific demands, which allowed flexibility and inclusiveness among participants. The many "Occupy movements" of 2011 in particular sought to "both transform the economic system to provide greater equality, opportunities, and personal fulfillment and, simultaneously, to democratize power in more participatory ways" (Tejerina et al. 2013: 377). These movements learned from each other in overlapping sequence, the Egyptians from the Tunisians, the Spanish from the Egyptians, and the Americans from the Spanish and the Egyptians (Romanos 2016).

The combination of favorable conditions with the direct participation and mentorship of veteran anarchists, many of whom had participated in Seattle, the Zapatista *encuentros*, or even decades earlier in New Left activism, injected an "anarchist DNA" into the mobilizations (Milkman et al. 2012; Williams 2012). As a result, there was an even greater deepening of shared commitment to horizontality, more inclusive participatory politics, and the establishment of prefigurative communities based on principles of mutual aid (Sitrin 2012; Williams 2012; Benski et al. 2013; Bray 2013; Schneider 2013; Graeber 2014; Hammond 2015).

Perhaps the most characteristic element of the Occupy movement and other "movements of the squares" in 2011 was the "reclaiming of the commons," enacted as the popular takeover of both public and private properties to establish temporary encampments (Abellán et al. 2012; Tejerina et al. 2013; van de Sande 2013; Sitrin 2020). This occupation was not simply a visible act of defiance, but also served as way for "squares and plazas [to] become public spheres where people could not only share alternatives, if not counter-hegemonic discourse, information, viewpoints, and ideas, but also where they could develop a sense of community and incubate novel forms of collective projects and identities" (Tejerina et al. 2013: 382). The physical sharing of space also enabled experimentation with participatory democratic models and steps toward a new moral economy that would give democracy a "new meaning" as "a horizontal, deliberative, transparent, and participatory dialogue between 'common persons' ... [which] demonstrated that another way of engaging with the public sphere was possible" (Tejerina et al. 2013: 383).

Endowed with everything from fully functional kitchens and libraries to medical and technology stations, it was through these camps that participants could prefigure alternatives such as transformative social relations, values, everyday practices, and even new organizational structures (Maeckelbergh 2011, 2012; Milkman et al. 2012; Bray 2013; Schneider 2013; Graeber 2014; Hammond 2015; Yates 2015). As one participant in the catalytic Zuccotti Park site in New York City put it: "Some of the old Socialist and Communist Parties were there, but they really weren't relevant. No one was looking to them for answers. It felt like what we were doing was something much fresher."[17]

Another participant in the meetings that led to Occupy described the origins of that movement specifically as a break from twentieth-century-style Communist party models:

> when Adbusters called for people to try to occupy Wall Street, the first people to show up were a bunch of Leninists, and it could have gone a very different way. The anarchists eventually broke off . . . and said "hey, we're just going to have our own meeting *over here*." That other meeting became the general assembly, which became Occupy Wall Street.[18]

Akin to the alter-globalization movement, however, certainly not all Occupy participants embraced the anarchist label, even while adopting anarchist principles. In fact, one former Occupier describes the participants as socialists engaging in practices imbued with anarchist ethics:

> I mean, let's be honest – all of us in Occupy were socialists in some way – but the space itself was anarchist, we were coming together and trying to take care of each other and ourselves in this community without capitalism, without exchanging money, everyone just doing their part . . . it was about [mutual aid] and how to create a community that cares and helps each other survive down to providing the basic things like clothes, food, staying warm . . . and at the same time, helping each other to survive emotionally and psychically.[19]

To another participant, labels were less important than vision and praxis: "I'm not particularly interested in what people call themselves – it's more what their views are and how they translate them into action."[20] In Occupy, this practice is considered by many activists and scholars to be a form of anarchism in action.

3.5 The Global North: Anarchist Politics in the USA and Beyond

Since the Occupy mobilizations of 2011, which saw the establishment of more than 1,500 camps in close to 80 countries (Langman and Benski 2013: 382), anarchism has continued to gain legitimacy in radical movements, and anarchist practices have widely diffused throughout the Left and popular culture in the Global North. As Grubačić commented reflecting on activism of the twenty-first century: "[A]narchism, at least in Europe and the Americas, has by now taken the place Marxism once occupied in the social movements of the 1960s."

---

[17] Unpublished interview by Benjamin Case, December 2014.

[18] Unpublished interview by Benjamin Case, November 2014.

[19] Unpublished interview with a Pittsburgh-based Occupier by Hillary Lazar, January 2017.

[20] Unpublished interview with a Pittsburgh-based Occupier by Hillary Lazar, May 2017.

As a core revolutionary ideology, it is the source of ideas and inspiration, and even those who do not consider themselves anarchists feel they have to define themselves in relation to it (Blumenfeld et al. 2013: 198). A "radical shift" that James Blumenfeld further observes can "be explained with reference to one verb: 'Occupy'" (Blumenfeld et al. 2013: 238). It comes as no surprise that as the movement waned, Occupiers carried many of these anarchist principles such as direct democracy, prefigurative politics, and mutual aid with them into other activist projects, mobilizations, and antifascist resistance. So, too, did the Spanish *indignados* and other participants from movements in the squares (Flesher Fominaya 2020; Sitrin 2020).

Mutual aid, as elaborated by Russian anarchist Peter Kropotkin,[21] is one of the clearest areas where the enduring and growing impact of anarchism on contemporary activism may be seen. For today's anarchists, mutual aid is practiced through locally rooted community support projects such as childcare collectives, community gardens, bail funds, and grocery and resource sharing. Mutual aid also has a long and deep tradition among Black, immigrant, and low-income communities, which is distinct from anarchism (Williams 2015; Spade 2020b; Lazar 2023). Yet they are related, in what William Anderson and Zoé Samudzi call "the anarchism of Blackness," the condition of being bound by the laws of a state from which one is excluded from the social contract. "Due to this extra-state location," they argue that "Blackness is, in so many ways, anarchistic. African-Americans, as an ethno-social identity comprised of descendants of enslaved Africans, have innovated new cultures and social organizations much like anarchism would require us to do outside of state structures" (Anderson and Samudzi 2017: 77).

Relief efforts in response to increasingly severe climate disasters and COVID-19 have made mutual aid increasingly popular – and mainstream (della Porta 2022). Even before Occupy, the anarchist Common Ground Collective helped to bring mutual aid principles to national attention through its provision of critical disaster relief services for thousands of New Orleans residents in the wake of Hurricane Katrina in 2005 (Crow 2014). In 2012, anarchist politics were further embedded in movement norms when, following the eviction of protestors from New York's Occupy sites, former Occupiers engaged in a huge mutual-aid-based relief and rebuilding effort in response to Hurricane Sandy, dubbed Occupy Sandy (Jaleel 2013). This, in turn, grew into new movement organizations, networks, and initiatives such as Mutual Aid Disaster Relief, which has hundreds of groups listed as part of its network and actively promotes an anarchist-informed approach to community preparedness

---

[21] Contemporary anarchists are strongly inspired by Kropotkin's *Mutual Aid* (1902), in which he argues that cooperation is as evident in the natural world as competition and is key to species survival (Boggs 1977; Maeckelberg 2011, 2012; Yates 2015).

for climate disasters.[22] Implicitly, anarchist self-organization amid catastrophe is even more common (Solnit 2010).

During the European refugee crisis of 2015, Greece, home to Exarchia, the "anarchist neighborhood" in Athens known for its popular assemblies and collectively run social centers (Apoifis 2016), had an extensive network of mutual-aid-based relief initiatives, from housing to schools and medical clinics. Spain, too, has a strong tradition of mutual aid initiatives and neighborhood assemblies, which informed the M15 movement (Abellán et al. 2012). And, of course, in response to the COVID-19 pandemic, there was a massive surge of interest in mutual aid worldwide. As Ariel Aberg-Riger (2020) comments in her visual history: "2020 was a year of crisis. A year of isolation. A year of protest. And a year of mutual aid." From explicitly anarchist collectives to grassroots nonprofits, people in many places assessed needs, delivered groceries, made DIY (Do It Yourself) masks, and more and crowdfunded to keep community members in safe housing (Aberg-Riger 2020; Firth 2020; Spade 2020a, 2020b). The year 2022 saw numerous European mutual aid groups spring up to support the vast refugee flood displaced by the Russian invasion of Ukraine (Gelderloos 2022; Wordworth 2022).

More subtle than the influence of specific aspects of anarchist politics is a more general move away from organizational hierarchies and formal political leadership on the Left. During the previous transnational revolutionary upsurge of the 1960s and 70s, many Left movements such as Civil Rights, Black Power, Women's Liberation, and various national liberation struggles were challenging the hierarchies they inherited from previous generations of movements and experimenting with internally participatory democracy. Yet many organizations typically still had formal structures and people in charge. In the USA, Students for a Democratic Society elected presidents, and the Student Nonviolent Coordinating Committee had a chairperson, as did the Black Panther Party. The function of these positions was not simply to facilitate meetings or represent members to the public; they were frequently ranking authoritative leaders. Behind these leaders were other ideological leaders – Lenin, Mao, and Guevara (Elbaum 2018). Or, perhaps, Martin Luther King, Jr., Elijah Muhammad, and Malcolm X. In cases such as various Communist parties or the Nation of Islam, leadership was largely beyond question or reproach.

Today, most people would be hard-pressed to name a single leader of any significant leftist organization, formation, or party, never mind leaders who have the authority to make decisions for groups. In the USA, even explicitly Marxist groups like the Democratic Socialists of America (DSA), Left Roots,

---

[22] https://mutualaiddisasterrelief.org.

Socialist Alternative, and Party for Socialism and Liberation do not put forward individual leaders to direct political decisions and take responsibility for groups' stances. The International Socialist Organization, which was for years the largest Socialist party in the USA until its collapse in 2019, did have an internally hierarchical structure – which directly contributed to the organization's demise. In its final communication, the committee responsible for dissolving the party blamed "the impact of decades of undemocratic practices, including a hostility to caucuses and the self-organization of members of oppressed groups."[23]

In the west, the Communist parties of the twentieth century have by and large turned to liberal democracy or faded to near-irrelevance. That said, there are resurgent Socialist parties, including the US-based DSA, which tripled in membership to more than 85,000 members during Bernie Sanders' campaign.[24] The DSA exercises significant pressure on the left flank of the Democratic Party, and claims several members of the House of Representatives as supporters (Swann 2017). The organization has a largely decentralized structure, based on internal democracy, and with each branch retaining a high degree of autonomy over its internal processes and local priorities.[25] And although there is central leadership in the form of elected committees, there is no single leader who wields power.[26] It is also notable that the DSA's Libertarian Socialist Caucus is explicitly composed of "syndicalists, council communists, anarchists, cooperativists, and municipalists, among many others" and puts out a remarkably anarchist-resonant platform based on self-determination; freedom from hierarchy, domination, and coercion; understanding of shared struggle; and solidarity based in mutual aid."[27]

---

[23] "Taking Our Final Steps," published in 2019 in *Socialist Worker* (http://socialistworker.org/2019/04/19/taking-our-final-steps). Accessed January 29, 2021. Perhaps the sole exception today is the Revolutionary Communist Party (RCP), headed by Bob Avakian. However, despite its energetic activism in the 1980s (Elbaum 2018), the RCP has long since lost credibility. Indeed, the RCP's veneration of a single leader is among the elements making that group seem so outdated.

[24] DSA newsletter, November 2020 (www.dsusa.org/news/npc-newsletter-nov2020/). Accessed January 18, 2021.

[25] Based on interview data collected by Benjamin Case. See also the DSA's organization chart (www.dsausa.org/files/2020/07/National-DSA-Organization-Chart.jpg). Accessed January 18, 2021.

[26] At least some local chapters of the DSA reflect anarchist influence. The Pittsburgh chapter's "anti-capitalist book club" featured discussions of work by Emma Goldman, Zapatista Subcomandante Marcos, and Murray Bookchin. A DSA member in the "Anchorage" chapter, noted that "there is going to be a progressive revolution in the country and it's not going to be done exclusively through the ballot box ... the mutual aid of anarchy can have such a profound effect [showing solidarity] and working with regular people" (unpublished interview by Hillary Lazar, August 2018).

[27] See "DSA Libertarian Socialist Caucus" at https://dsa-lsc.org/.

The "ecosocialist" group Cooperation Jackson is one of the most advanced revolutionary projects in the USA, building for years a "dual power" strategy in Jackson, Mississippi (Akuno and Meyer 2023). Drawing from Black nationalist, socialist, feminist, and environmental justice traditions, Cooperation Jackson's concrete program contains the following points: "a federation of emerging local cooperatives"; development of community-controlled energy production; participatory budgeting; and "green worker cooperatives, a mutual aid network, and solidarity economy institutions" (Akuno and Meyer 2023: 26–28).

Today, there are activist celebrities and social media "influencers," but it is far more uncommon to find a group on the radical Left with a singular general secretary, field marshal, chairperson, or president who gives top-down orders to members or who dictates policies and political stances. If the 1960s global revolutionary era and the New Left that followed raised questions and challenged hierarchies on the Left, this trend became notably anarchist in character by the early twenty-first century. Anyone who learned what a Socialist party was from the pre–Second World War German Socialist Party or from the Russian Bolsheviks or from the Spanish Socialist and Communist parties that played key roles in Spain's post-Franco democratic transition would be astonished at how little socialist formations today resemble the top-down commanding structures of these organizations.[28]

Beyond nominally Socialist and Communist parties, we also see an eschewal of traditional leadership structures in the most significant political movements on the Left in the Global North in the last decade: the 2012 Quebec Student Protests; Gezi Park; Black Lives Matter (BLM); Extinction Rebellion; the French Yellow Vests (CrimethInc 2012, 2018, 2022; Abbas and Yigit 2015). And while some explicit anarchists were involved in these mobilizations – even in key roles – these mobilizations were not "anarchist-led." Rather they reflect a general shift toward horizontalism among today's movement groups and mobilizations (Berglund and Schmidt 2020). The emergence of formal hierarchy is widely perceived as a weakness and even a reason to leave a group or movement altogether.

Take BLM for example. Initially a Twitter hashtag and then organized as a coordinated but decentralized network, the group's membership overwhelmingly eschewed formal leadership, referring to themselves as horizontal and "leaderful" (see Barrón-López 2020; Wood 2020). After formalizing BLM as an organization, Alicia Garza, who first tweeted the phrase "Black Lives Matter," would step back from the movement to forestall becoming a leader over others,

---

[28] Accordingly, social movement scholars have been highlighting the importance of movement communities, not just movement organizations, as sources of solidarity, energy, and identity (e.g., Staggenborg 2002).

which to her would have distracted from the goals of the movement (Mahdawi 2020). When Patrisse Cullors, the last remaining founder in the BLM organization, made executive moves without consulting membership, ten chapters broke ties with the BLM Global Network in protest (see King 2020).

It is worth noting that anarchism has also diffused into mainstream culture. The sharing economy, for instance, a form of "compassionate capitalism," appeals to mutual aid and resource sharing. There has been a commodification of anarchist culture in mass marketed punk apparel and aesthetics. Villains in action movies and shows are frequently portrayed as anarchists or with anarchist symbols.[29] The youth magazine *Teen Vogue* regularly features incisive articles on anarchist politics and practices (e.g., Kelly 2020). And, within the academic sphere, scholars and academics have become increasingly interested in anarchist frameworks in their analyses.

Unsurprisingly, the anarchist turn has not gone unnoticed by governments and security agencies. In 2010, the FBI released a primer on anarchists as a domestic terrorist threat. A decade later, US President Donald Trump directed his Office of Management and Budget and his Attorney General to deny federal funds to the "anarchist jurisdictions" he claimed to be taking root in numerous American cities (Haberman and McKinley 2020). Despite noting the extreme rarity of lethality in anarchist actions, a 2021 report by the Center for Strategic and International Studies described militant anarchists as "a persistent threat that will challenge domestic security in the United States" (Hwang 2021). Although the anti-communist politics of the "Red Scare" continue to echo, the specter of revolution is becoming increasingly adorned with anarchist black flags.

3.6 The Global South: Anarchist Politics in Latin America and Beyond[30]

While the Zapatista revolt may have marked the ascendancy of anarchist practices and frameworks in transnational mobilizing, it was also only one instance of a broader cultural shift in the Latin American Left toward more anarchistic organizational models and ideas. Strongly hierarchical Left and expressly socialist organizations have given way to networks of activists disdainful of leaders and rigid hierarchies, committed to internal democratic debate, acting in local or transnational arenas as much as national ones, and

---

[29] For a few prominent examples, see the Batman film, *The Dark Knight* (2008); the Mission: Impossible movies, *Rogue Nation* (2015) and *Fallout* (2018); James Bond films, *The World Is Not Enough* (1999) and *No Time to Die* (2020); and *XXX* (2002). In 2022, HBO produced a docuseries called *The Anarchists*, which is actually about utopian free-market libertarians, but promoted the show using the name and imagery of leftwing anarchism.

[30] Parts of this section borrow from Burridge and Markoff (2023).

seeking to develop autonomy from established political and economic structures (Thwaites Rey 2011; Stahler-Sholk et al. 2014). Since the 1990s, along with the Zapatistas, myriad other indigenous, feminist, urban-based, and peasant movements have explicitly based their activism on both horizontalism and rejection of traditional political vehicles like unions, parties, and states (Zibechi 2010). Although many of these activists disavow the explicit anarchist label, their practices reflect anarchist values and overlap with explicitly anarchist movements.

Argentine mobilizations and the worker-run factories that emerged in response to the economic collapse of 2001 offer some of the most obvious examples. These takeovers reflected a general shift toward horizontalist strategies – seen in neighborhood assemblies (Auyero 2003), certain groups of *piqueteros* (blockers of roads) (Rossi 2017), movements for community-based schools (Heidemann 2018), and alternative human rights organizations (Sitrin 2014b). Initially driven by necessity as owners sought to close shops amid economic crisis, workers in many factories and other businesses responded by assuming all aspects of management in addition to production. Notably, this was not the result of planning by an established leadership, but rather grew from workers' mutual aid and direct action in a formal power vacuum, which led to the discovery of new forms of collective power. Although these groups have important linkages to Peronists and Trotskyists, the grassroots organizing principles adopted were very much in line with anarchist practices. The recuperated workplaces have inspired workers' movements throughout the world, and it is from Argentina that "horizontalism" has entered the tactical vocabulary of transnationally connected activists (Sitrin 2014b).

Bolivia offers another case. In the 2004 "Water War" in Cochabamba, Bolivia, successful resistance to water privatization was impelled by grassroots assemblies with rotating leaderships housed in already-existing community organizations. This enabled rapid collective decision-making and an effective, citywide mobilization (Olivera 2004). Meanwhile, the Aymara-dominated Bolivian city of El Alto has long demonstrated the grassroots power of autonomist and horizontalist politics. Here, the city's neighborhood associations (*Federación de Juntas Vecinales de El Alto* [FEJUVES]) are contemporary manifestations of the *ayllu*, the primary historical unit of Aymara organization.[31] The FEJUVES embody direct participation and horizontal

---

[31] Following Zibechi (2010), Hylton and Thompson (2007), and Rivera Cusicanqui (2015), we can see how Aymara social organization based on the *ayllu* (as well as *ejido* collective land holdings in Zapatista-held Chiapas) demonstrates that current expressions of resistance and self-government in the Americas are just as deeply rooted in *non-liberal* forms of collective organization as they are in western liberal democratic values. Indeed, non-liberal social forms

organization, facilitated by the dispersion of power among all community members through rotating, compulsory leadership (Zibechi 2010: 14–15). This dispersed political organization facilitated the autonomous control of urban neighborhoods that was crucial in the "Gas Wars" of 2003 and 2005 and the toppling of two governments in those same years (Zibechi 2010: 45–46). And while many of these FEJUVES were eventually demobilized, diluted, or otherwise co-opted by the Movimiento al Socialismo (MAS) governments of Evo Morales (Dangl 2010; Oikonomakis and Espinoza 2014; Brown 2020), subsequent popular discontent with the failure of Morales' party to implement the full extent of its initially transformative agenda in El Alto and elsewhere has led some sectors within the FEJUVES of El Alto to return to prioritizing horizontalist linkages and decolonizing practices in their means of communication, organizational structures, and local economies (Brown 2020; Chandler 2021).

We can see similar anarchist-aligned practices in still other Latin American examples. In civil-war-torn Colombia, the vitiated peacemaking process of 2016 was initially deepened and radicalized by the intensive mobilization of autonomous social movements in the streets, in occupied public spaces, and in the halls of power where peace talks were occurring. This diverse group of movements (feminist, indigenous, youth, and student groups) proved to be a thorn in the side of the government negotiation team, as they refused to send "leaders" or "representatives" to negotiate with the government in the context of peace talks, depriving the process itself of legitimacy.[32] And in Nicaragua, the concentration of "leftist" Sandinista power into an authoritarian, bureaucratic state machine led by President Daniel Ortega and his wife and Vice President Rosario Murillo marginalized and radicalized many Left movements that had previously operated in close collaboration with the Sandinista party (Almeida 2014). Even before the "civic insurrection" of April 2018 (Sanchez and Osorio Mercado 2020), feminist, environmental, and cooperative movements had already begun organizing outside of traditional state and party structures, relying on decentralized, territorialized practices and endogenous resources as opposed to the government or international cooperation. René Mendoza, an agricultural technician with the Winds of Peace Foundation, describes the "silent movement" in the Nicaraguan countryside, organized

---

have direct affinities with anarchist values of localized collective rule and popular control over delegates or representatives. Engaging with and theorizing the practices of ordinary "non-western" peoples contributes to understanding the history of anarchy in practice as well as its present popularity in terms of "use value" for facilitating human survival and flourishing in response to the interlocking crises of established power structures.

[32] We thank Natalia Duarte for these observations.

along cooperative and kinship networks and grounded in "autonomous thought"[33].

Haydee Castillo, now exiled in Miami after persecution for her role in anti-government protests in 2018–2019, but formerly the President of Foro de Mujeres Para la Integración Centroamericana y Del Caribe, provided a similar perspective from a feminist movement. She spoke of an emerging awareness that the Sandinista Revolution of 1979 occurred within a patriarchal and authoritarian political culture that only intensified within the ruling party upon its return to state power in 2006.[34] She stated that this has "caused the values of the Left to come into dispute" and went on: "I think we are watching an old part [of the Left] die and a new part emerging, where we need to see a visionary, strategic, honorable, and horizontal leadership – to no longer do things how we used to … a new way to exercise power, another way to construct political culture, and a repositioning of values." Referring to her territorial organizing work in the northernmost rural regions of the country, Castillo observed that "In the Segovias, we have begun to talk about self-governance, and that is where the hope of the people is: we can no longer think about depending on the national government …." In the historic colonial city of León, Mujeral en Acción, a group of feminist activists has coalesced around horizontalist and feminist "self-management" in which they work to protect and advocate for women's sexual and reproductive rights through direct support and mutual aid for women victims of violence. They have a volunteer-based model of self-management and self-financing as opposed to any formal or legal organizational structure. And they pool time and resources to provide workshops, raise community awareness, and provide other forms of direct support to survivors.

Along with the implicit anarchist presence in contemporary Latin America, there are also many examples of explicit anarchist efforts, particularly in urban centers like Buenos Aires or Montevideo, whose anarchist history dates back to the European immigration of the nineteenth century (Cappelletti 1995). In Bolivia, Mujeres Creando was an anarcha-feminist group that was active at the turn of the millennium (Ainger 2002). Larger networked organizations include: Federación Anarco-Comunista de Argentina founded in 2010; Federación Liberteria de Argentina dating back to the 1930s and connected to the International of Anarchist Federations; Fórum do Anarquismo Organizado in Brazil that was active from 2002 to 2010 and Federação Anarquista do Rio de Janeiro that has been active since 2003; and the Federación Comunista Libertaria in Chile that was established in 2011 when several Chilean anarcho-

---

[33] Unpublished interview by Daniel Burridge, Carretera a Masaya, Nicaragua, October 16, 2017.
[34] Unpublished interview by Daniel Burridge, León, Nicaragua, August 11, 2016.

communist groups decided to merge, to name just a few. Anarchist organizers and models were also key in Brazil's Free Transportation Movement in 2013 and anti-World Cup protests in 2014 (Dupuis-Déri 2019).

In Cuba, home to perhaps the most durable state Socialist experiment in the world, anarchists represent the main movement challenge from the Left.[35] While US-based media make it appear that discontent with the Cuban government is synonymous with pro-US and pro-market forces, protests on the island are resisting increasingly calcified power structures and rising economic inequality – precisely the same conditions the Left is fighting in countries around the world. Much like anarchists elsewhere, Cuban anarchists agitate around the need for freedom from global capitalism, in this case enforced by their own Socialist government (Taller Libertario Alfredo López 2021). As in other Latin American countries ruled by nominal leftists, anarchists in Cuba represent an existential challenge, criticizing regimes for their failure to live up to revolutionary principles and belying regime characterization of all dissent as pro-US. Perhaps acknowledging their political and cultural salience, the Cuban government has repeatedly responded by claiming "real anarchists" support the government, while only "false anarchists" protest, attempting to claim anarchism as its own, a move that Cuban anarchists fiercely resist (Uzcategui 2017).

As in other world regions, we can observe across Latin America, the prevalence of transnational organizing in which activists increasingly link local and national struggles across borders (Smith and Wiest 2012). The anti-mining movement in El Salvador – a horizontalist assemblage of diverse organizations (Spalding 2014) – is connected transnationally to other environmental movements in the Alianza Centroamericana Frente a la Minería. Transnationally linked indigenous organizations such as the Foro Indígena de Abya Yala, the Foro de Comunicación Indígena, and the Coordinadora Andina de Organizaciones Indígenas have contributed to the crystallization of a hemispheric agenda for indigenous peoples' cultural, social, and political revitalization. Feminist movements, even those as locally focused as Mujeral, have also focused on transnational sites of movement building such as participation in the World March of Women, and numerous regional articulations.

It is by no means only in Latin America that mobilizations of the Global South are drawing on anarchist playbooks. The Rojava Revolution is one of the clearest recent manifestations of the anarchist turn. Occurring amidst the Syrian civil war engendered by Arab Spring protests, it is considered by many explicit anarchists "as one of the most important revolutions in history" and akin to what

---

[35] Anarchists, in fact, played an early and significant part in shaping leftist politics on the island (Shaffner 2019).

the Zapatista uprising was at the turn of the millennium for a new generation of radicals (Villanueva 2018). During the Syrian civil war of 2012–2013, Abdullah Öcalan, jailed leader of the Kurdistan Workers' Party in Turkey, was inspired by Murray Bookchin's libertarian communalism and, in turn, helped inspire in Rojava arguably the most extensive social anarchist experiment (Bookchin and Biehl 1998; Graeber 2014; Potiker 2019). Along with emphasizing direct democracy practiced through the establishment of more than 200 cooperatives and thousands of communes and collectives, it is also known for the feminist initiatives evident in its numerous women's councils and cooperatives[36] as well as its formidable units of armed women (Leverink 2015; Strangers in a Tangled Wilderness 2015; Knapp et al. 2016). The creation of what amounts to an anarchist counter-state in war-torn Kurdistan, caught between hostile governments in Syria, the forces of the Islamic State to the South, and those of Turkey to the North, has inspired supporters to travel from all corners of the world to fight on a scale not seen on the Left since the Spanish Revolution.

Asef Bayat (2021: 225–226) describes how in the wake of Arab Spring, Black Bloc activism emerged among poor young men "in eight Egyptian cities, in the streets, and across several dozen Facebook pages," and how the Tunisian group Feminism Attack took on "anarchist practices." Anarchist clubs of "football hooligans" with their own transnational alliances and experience fighting the police took frontline positions in squaring off against security forces in Egypt during the 2011 January Revolution (Malsin 2013). The years of Palestine solidarity efforts reflect both the participation of anarchists, such as the Israeli group Anarchists Against the Wall, as well as anarchistic values and tactics (Gordon 2009, 2010; Williams 2018). And echoes of Rojava could be heard in the decentralized, widespread, and leaderful movements spearheaded by Iranian women that began in 2022.

Other examples abound. Anarchist protest practices were prominent in Hong Kong's democratic Umbrella Movement in 2019 (CrimethInc 2019) and Nigeria's "EndSARS" anti-police uprising in 2020. Few activists in Nigeria used the label "anarchist," though it was widely applied as a term of derision by the government (Guardian Nigeria 2020). Anarchist movement histories in Africa more broadly, as well as small-a anarchist traditional practices across the continent, have been largely erased from radical histories, but their effects are not insignificant (Mbah and Igariwey 1997). In late 2019, an outburst of student activism against fascism in India employed horizontal models and took autonomous direct action (Mishra 2019). Commenting on

---

[36] The Rojava Revolution has not only captured media and popular attention but also inspired new movement organizations like the Revolutionary Abolitionist Movement, which combines Black Liberation struggles, Rojava democratic confederalism, and armed community defense.

the Indian student struggles, journalist Pankaj Mishra notes that there has been a "global wildfire of street protests, from Sudan to Chile, Lebanon to Hong Kong [that] has finally reached the country whose 1.3 billion population is mostly below the age of 25." As he sees it, especially for these young activists:

> Old-style political parties and movements are in disarray; societies, more polarized than ever before; and the young have never faced a more uncertain future. As angry, leaderless individuals revolt against increasingly authoritarian states and bureaucracies from Santiago to New Delhi, anarchist politics seems an idea whose time has come. (2019)

Furthermore, many of the trends we identify in the Global North are also evident in parts of the Global South. In the last decade, there have been many examples of mutual-aid-based disaster relief efforts, including Typhoon Yolanda in the Philippines in 2013 and earthquakes in Mexico in 2017 (Firth 2020). During the peak of the COVID-19 pandemic, robust mutual aid efforts sprang up in every part of the world, from Taiwan to South Africa to Iraq (Sitrin and Colectiva Sembrar 2020). To be sure, mutual aid, like other anarchist principles we are discussing, does not belong to anarchists alone. In many instances, however, self-identifying anarchists played prominent roles in these initiatives (Sitrin and Colectiva Sembrar 2020; Firth 2020). Paralleling our earlier discussion of twenty-first-century movement organizations in the Global North lacking a singular commanding leader, Bamyeh (2023) has argued that revolutionary movements in the Global South have come to be characterized by the absence of a charismatic figure backed by a vanguard party and provides valuable empirical instantiations from the Middle East and North Africa. All this is further evidence that collective action adopting anarchistic practices is far more widespread than that label.

3.7 Across the world, the anarchist practice of uprisings

One of the most dramatic global expressions of anarchist politics is the increasing prevalence of spontaneous uprisings across the world. At the dawn of the twenty-first century, scholars were already noting a shift toward sudden outbursts of civil rebellion (Foran 2003). In the neoliberal, urbanized context of the decades that followed, mass uprisings have come to dominate social movement contention, typically in the form of unexpected and rapidly escalating civilian-based mobilizations and occupations of public space by previously unorganized populations (Bayat 2017). A recent event-level study of nearly 3,000 protests from 900 movements across the world found that recent years have seen dramatic increases of mass social unrest in every region (Ortiz et al. 2021). Not only are protests growing in number and size across the world – some uprisings have been among the largest in each country's recent history – but they have often erupted suddenly, their numbers swelled by political newcomers, not drawn from longstanding organizations and political parties but "unorganized citizens, grassroots movements, and young and old persons" (Ortiz et al. 2021: 4).

Several of the episodes mentioned earlier, like the Arab Spring and Occupy movements of 2011, are prime examples of this kind of rupture. But whereas we previously discussed the politics and practices of activists in these moments, here we highlight the tactical nature of the uprisings themselves. Indeed, as much as diffusion of any particular labels or organizational practices, it is the "anarchist method" (Bamyeh 2013) of these uprisings that has caught on – civil revolts involving mass demonstrations, unarmed fights with armed security forces, and experimentation with living revolution through encampments occupying public space.

While many anarchists also advocate for the types of slow-burn labor and community organizing that Marxists and other leftists emphasize, anarchists have distinguished themselves in their articulated agitation for spontaneous mass revolt in recent generations – for leaderless (or as many prefer, leaderful) insurrections. Civil uprisings of the twenty-first century have been predominantly spontaneous and horizontal, not strategically orchestrated by parties or organizations but rather sparked by outrage over corruption and police violence, their politics emergent from participants' collective actions and discussions. This type of revolt forced itself into popular consciousness in 2011 but has only multiplied in number and scale since then. In 2019 alone, there were mass civilian uprisings in Algeria, Bolivia, Chile, Colombia, Ecuador, Egypt, France, Georgia, Haiti, Hong Kong, Iran, Iraq, Lebanon, Peru, Poland, Puerto Rico, Russia, Sudan, and Zimbabwe. Some managed to topple governments in a few weeks, and others significantly influenced policy outcomes and political conditions. Some, failing at displacing tyrants from national power, left a cultural legacy (Bayat 2021), the effects of which might not be fully known until the next moment of uprising. Crucially, *none of these insurrections emerged from or led to unified political parties, nor followed or produced singular leaders.*

In many ways, the organized Left has been forced to play catch-up to twenty-first century revolts. The George Floyd Uprising was catalyzed by a viral cell phone video of then-officer Derek Chauvin murdering Black Minneapolis resident George Floyd – and by riots that subsequently burned down the Minneapolis Third Precinct. In a matter of days, demonstrators were on the streets of every US state and well beyond, amounting to the largest protest mobilizations in US history, and arguably the largest global uprising on behalf of racial justice, reaching over sixty countries (Buchanan et al. 2020; Vortex Group 2023). For many of these protests, it was locals, young people, and political newcomers who organized and animated most actions, and especially the more riotous ones. This dynamic is the new norm for mass movements. This is not to say prior organizing is not crucial, nor is it to claim that parties or personalities do not attempt to capitalize on insurrections' momentum afterwards. Nor are the uprisings typically organized by self-described anarchists, but the anarchist tenor of a horizontal, bottom-up, and direct action approach is unmistakable (Graeber 2008).

The lack of centrally organized leadership in these uprisings has not meant lack of coordination. No sooner had the BLM uprising hit the streets in Ferguson than Palestinian activists were posting tips on how to deal with tear gas and militarized police repression (Jackson 2016). During their uprising in 2019, Hong Kong activists and US-based anarchists traded tactical toolkits (Anonymous 2019). The "black bloc" tactic that for some has become synonymous with anarchist protests in the US was itself adopted from European autonomists (Dupuis-Déri 2014). Intrastate and transnational cooperation and coordination may even be enhanced by the lack of parties and leaders, whose political calculations and squabbles can cause downstream rifts for entire movements. Instead, collaboration is driven by well-established values of solidarity, autonomy, and mutual aid.

4 Explaining the Anarchist Turn

We have seen considerable evidence for an anarchist turn in many places in the late twentieth and early twenty-first centuries. Why? A satisfactory explanation needs to account for several things. It needs to cover a very broad geography, not just developments in particular countries. Otherwise, it cannot explain how the linguistic trend is notable in the multicontinental languages of English, Spanish, and French, and how the practical trends are exhibited by movements across geographic regions. Any explanation also needs to account for why the linguistic shift began between the 1960s and the 1980s (depending on the language), then generally continued to grow across decades and jumped notably higher from the 1990s into the present century – and how the trend of anarchist practices appears to have accelerated in the twenty-first century. Finally, an explanation does not just need to account for an anarchist turn but for its amplitude. Qualitative research indicates the near ubiquity of anarchistic qualities and practices in many of the most consequential movements in recent decades, and in most languages the relative salience of anarchism to socialism is even greater in the early twenty-first century than it had been in the 1960s and 1970s, with a parallel acceleration in the newspaper data. Twenty-first century anarchism has drawn on many radical currents, not only the anarchist past; it is a notable presence alongside others in many movements; and it has influenced many activists who do not call themselves anarchists.

Our proposed explanation has four sections:

First, we will point to widespread and growing discontent with dominant political, economic, and social models, as the forms of liberal democracy spread as never before in human history. At the same time, state management of economies that had developed in many countries after the Second World War gave way to the elevation of the (so-called) free market to institutional domination across much of the planet, a new pattern its critics called "neoliberalism."

Second, the increasing human costs of this combination of democracy and neoliberalism, experienced in countries with very different histories of democracy, levels of wealth, and power in the world, increasingly fueled longing and hope for something radically different. In this context, anarchism has been attractive for both negative and positive reasons. *Negatively*, other strategies for radical social transformation had become unattractive, and increasingly unattractive at that. Those hoping for radical change have historically embraced a variety of strategies, some of which had become less able to inspire, and particularly so since the decades beginning in the 1970s. With some past roads to a better future looking less promising, or even hazardous, radical activists sought other paths, increasingly imbuing movements with an "anarchist sensibility" (Epstein (2001: 1).

Third – and *positively* – anarchist visions of a better world spoke more and more to the problems of our global age, including the question of what democracy might mean in an interconnected world and how one might bring about alternatives to capitalism in practice today.

Fourth, we see a confluence of several streams that have helped to deepen the "small-a" anarchism of contemporary activism. The legacy of the 1960s and 1970s meant many anarchist ideas were familiar in radical culture, while new communications technologies made it easier to adopt certain anarchist practices, cross-pollination of movements, and the emergence of transnational, global cultures of protest. Finally, the "anarchist spirit" evident in the many spontaneous uprisings speaks to a shared feeling of urgency in response to ever-growing economic inequality, the beginnings of climate collapse, endemic state violence, and systematic devaluation of Black, brown, and indigenous peoples across the world. This urgency grows greater with the need to combat resurgent Far-Right movements devoted to returning to a world in which women stayed in their limited place, queer people were out of sight, white men ran the world, and colonized peoples stayed in the colonies.

4.1 Why Are Protestors Calling for Radical Change?

4.1.1 Democracy Disappoints

Starting with Portugal, Greece, and Spain in the 1970s, there was an enormous increase in the number of democratic countries in the world, an upward trend that continued into the early twenty-first century. By the early 1990s, some were proclaiming that the progression of history was essentially over – that the struggle for democracy had been achieved in much of the world, and that the rest of the world would sooner or later catch up. In a 1989 essay titled "The End of History?" Francis Fukuyama asked if what he saw as a long struggle between democracy and noxious alternatives had been won. Three years later, he dropped the question mark in the book title (Fukuyama 1992).

But also in the 1990s, political scientists began to notice a great deal of discontent with democratic institutions in practice in country after country – and not only where democracy was newly installed, or shaky, or dubious, but also in countries of long-standing democratic practice (Clarke et al. 1995; Nye et al. 1997; Norris 1999; Pharr and Putnam 2000). The United States was early to generate scholarly attention on this point (Lipset and Schneider 1983). And researchers soon noted something similar in Canada (Adams and Lennon 1992) and then in Europe (Norris 1999). Dalton summarized this research early in the new century: "By almost any measure, public confidence and trust in, and support, for politicians, political parties, and political institutions has eroded over the past generation" (2004: 191).[37]

Research from the 2010s shows a continuation. Larry Diamond's (2019: 154–160) review of public opinion surveys conducted between 2014 and 2017 in Latin America, Asia, Africa, and the Middle East can be summed up as the following: large majorities claim to strongly favor democracy in the abstract, many people in many countries are extremely critical of how their own democratic government works in practice, and growing minorities are becoming indifferent to or even favorable to some authoritarian alternative. Let us follow Diamond (2019: 159) taking note of Tunisia. This was the only Arab country that became and remained democratic for at least several years as a consequence of the upheavals of the Arab Spring in 2011. According to Arab Barometer (2019), Tunisians in 2018 overwhelmingly held that "democracy, despite its problems, is the best political system": 79 percent agreed, somewhat down from 85 percent two years earlier, though still higher than in the pivotal year of 2011. But positive responses to "how much trust do you have in the government" have eroded radically with experience of democracy: from 62 percent in 2011 down to 20 percent in 2018. Suggestive of

---

[37] But see Norris (2011) for significant qualifications.

the future, trust in government is notably lower among young adults.[38] Many of the disillusioned were pleased when, in July 2021, Tunisia's president ignored parliament and seized power; when a plaque celebrating the 2011 democratic revolution was damaged in a Tunis suburb, no one cared to fix it (Yee 2021).

As for the wealthy and apparently secure democracies of Western Europe and North America, the data is also alarming. Roberto Stefan Foa and Yascha Mounk (2016) examine the World Values Surveys from 2005 through 2014 for European Union member states and the USA. A majority of Europeans and a very large majority of Americans born before Second World War, asked to rate on a scale from 1 to 10 how "essential" is living "in a democracy," respond with a maximal 10. But those figures are vastly different among younger generations, with only about 30 percent of US millennials giving that response. Rising numbers in both the USA and Europe respond that democracy is a "bad" or "very bad" way to "run this country" (Foa and Mounk 2016: 7, 9).[39]

The Centre for the Future of Democracy at the University of Cambridge recently published the results of a truly enormous study of democratic legitimacy in the world based on data from 4.8 million respondents in 160 countries from 1973 into 2020 that show young people are increasingly dissatisfied with democracy, in Latin America, Sub-Saharan Africa, Western Europe, and the "Anglo-Saxon" democracies. Exceptionally, in Eastern Europe, satisfaction with democracy was rising (though the research was conducted before Russia invaded Ukraine) but remained at low levels (Foa et al. 2020).

These trends in the survey data are matched by other evidence that the global burst of democratization has given way to de-democratization by conventional measures. According to Freedom House's 2019 annual report on the state of democracy (Repucci 2020), democracy had been in decline in the world from 2006 on, with more countries each year decreasing on their measures. Meriting special attention for their contribution to this trend in 2019 were Benin, El Salvador, India, Mauritania, Myanmar, Senegal, Thailand, and the United States. Of the forty-one countries classified as "established democracies" because they had democratic systems for two decades prior to 2006, twenty-five "suffered overall declines" (Repucci 2020: 10). This report groups countries into six world-regions and every one of them saw notable declines in democracy (Repucci 2020: 12). But there has been important democratic activism, too; 2019 was a year of "mass protests … in every region of the world" (Repucci 2020: 13). Among places named as sites of large pro-democracy protest are Hong Kong, Bolivia, Sudan, Chile, Algeria, Iran, Russia, India, and Ethiopia.

---

[38] The specific data cited are from Arab Barometer (2019: 5–7, 12).

[39] For debate about these findings, see Inglehart (2016) and Mounk (2018: 105–122).

As for the USA, in the presidential elections of 2020, 74.2 million citizens voted for Donald Trump, 11.3 million more than had voted for him in 2016, not repelled by four years of displays of his contempt for dissent, press freedoms, reasoned debate, and democracy (not to mention racism, misogyny, narcissism, nepotism, self-dealing, and other forms of corruption, cruelty, lying, and incompetence). In a country that has long claimed to be a beacon of democracy in the world, that is a lot of people indifferent or hostile to some democratic future. According to the Pew Research Center (2021) survey, only about one-fifth of Americans "say they can trust the government in Washington to do what is right 'just about always' (2%) or 'most of the time' (22%)." A recent study of thousands of protest events across the globe between 2006 and 2020 also found that the central issues driving the worldwide rise in protests and protesters are "failures of democracy and of economic and social development, fueled by discontent and lack of faith in the official political processes" (Ortiz et al. 2021: 2). Scholars from diverse academic fields took note of such currents, and added to the sense of democratic malaise, with what amounted to a literary subgenre of books on how democracy goes to hell.[40]

4.2 Why This Democratic Malaise?

Opinion surveys in many countries, scholarly reflection, and measures of the state of democracy converge on acute doubt about whether current political models are adequate for addressing the challenges of our historical moment. Some hope to bring about radical change, and, as we have seen in the first section of this Element, there are substantial empirical grounds for seeing much of this radicalism as anarchistic. To address phenomena occurring across geographies and changing over time, we need an explanation that is both global and temporal.

4.2.1 We Start with the Dynamics of Democracy

Since its birth in the revolutionary big bang at the end of the eighteenth century, modern democracy has nurtured social movements challenging the democracy thus far achieved. Claiming to be the rule of "the people," democracy legitimated ordinary people finding their voice, often loudly. By making elections the

---

[40] Some titles as examples: *Can Democracy Survive Global Capitalism?*; *How Democracies Die*; *Can Democracy be Saved?*; *Ill Winds: Saving Democracy from Russian Rage, Chinese Ambition, and American Complacency*; *The Light that Failed: Why the West Is Losing the Fight for Democracy*; *The People vs. Democracy: Why our Freedom Is in Danger and How to Save It*; *The Global Rise of Authoritarianism in the 21st Century: Crisis of Neoliberal Globalization and the Nationalist Response*; *The Road to Unfreedom: Russia, Europe, America*; *How Democracy Ends*; *If We Can Keep It: How the Republic Collapsed and How It Might Be Saved*; *Cultural Backlash: Trump, Brexit and Authoritarian Populism*; *Degenerations of Democracy*; *Crises of Democracy*; and just plain *Crisis*.

linchpin of gaining formal power, democratic governance embodied protections for the formation and action of organizations to contest power. In addition, the claim that power is accountable to the "people" constrains use of the tools of repression, though hardly eliminates it – but the repression itself can be contested.

Finally, but importantly, the expansive promises of democracy are both contradictory and unfulfilled. This means that democracy in practice is often infuriating to the exploited, marginalized, and oppressed, who long for frequently proclaimed but unrealized democratic principles. Nothing is more galvanizing than democracy's broken promises (Markoff 2019), including foundational claims of broad inclusion and social equality, falsified from the beginning of modern democracy by exclusions and inequalities and, therefore, a common theme of challenging social movements (Markoff 2011). So, movements rejecting existing social arrangements are built into the DNA of democracy. Challenging existing democracy in the name of democracy is a permanent source of dynamism. Movements of "outrage and hope," as Manuel Castells (2012) characterized the multicountry rebellions of 2011, were not rare in democratic history long before that date and will continue into any democratic future, too. But why are radical challenges especially salient in recent decades?

4.2.2 This brings us to the dynamics of capitalism

It is no secret that the practices that get summed up as "capitalism" amount to a challenge both to age-old lifeways and to its own recently implanted habits and recent adaptations to the last set of changes. Capitalism incessantly revolutionizes everything. Here is the classic formulation:

> All fixed, fast-frozen relations, with their train of ancient and venerable prejudices and opinions, are swept away, all new-formed ones become antiquated before they can ossify. All that is solid melts into air, all that is holy is profaned, and man is at last compelled to face with sober senses his real conditions of life, and his relations with his kin. (Marx and Engels 1848)

Capitalism has had periods in which inequalities in income and wealth were decreasing (as in the USA between the 1930s and the 1980s), but since the 1980s, the grand trend has been increasing inequalities, and in countries like the United States, sharply (Piketty 2017). One of the variables most strongly correlated with the youth dissatisfaction with democracy that we noted in section headed "Democracy Disappoints" is their country's level of income inequality (Foa et al. 2020: 16–17). There is also a venerable argument that capitalism sets limits to whatever egalitarian possibilities are opened by enlarged rights of suffrage, a proposition that has received extensive discussion (e.g., Przeworski 2010: 66–98; Wright 2010: 337–365). In this argument, one of the infuriating contradictory features of democracy is these limits, which reliably makes democracy's claims of equality among citizens a recurrent source of outrage to those offended by actual inequalities. To these general propensities of capitalism to generate grievances that can fuel movements for change, we add a specific recent galvanizing moment, the Great Recession of 2008–2009. No one could credibly discuss the explosive protest movements of 2011 in Greece, Spain, and the United States without highlighting the Great Recession, which gets us from capitalism's radicalism-generating cyclical downturns across centuries to the neoliberalism of recent decades.

4.2.3 Neoliberalism

The First World War, the Great Depression, and the Second World War: each of these periods of intense human suffering and social dislocation impelled a big leap in the intensity of state management of economic life, to keep productivity geared to sustaining the wars, and to dampen the downside of the capitalist business cycle. After the First World War, moreover, the Soviet Union's new revolutionary government set about eliminating capitalism, including the role of the private marketplace; after the Second World War, an extended Soviet Bloc adopted similar policies. Meanwhile, some of the wealthier capitalist countries had been trying to tame the market in the face of massive unemployment and unused industrial capacity during the Great Depression, questioning previous confidence in the untrammeled marketplace. After the Second World War, many of those countries significantly expanded or established social safety nets to undercut the appeals of the Soviet model as well as local Left radicalism whether allied or opposed to the Soviet Union. And in that postwar era, governments in Latin America and in some of the countries newly independent of colonial masters gravitated toward a Third World developmentalism, in which tariffs would protect national industry following a strategy of import substitution while social safety nets and subsidies (e.g., keeping bus fare low) would support a growing working class for local factories. In these ways, a variety of paths converged on a sense that the state should in some way guide economic policy even in peacetime. A smart state, relying on economists on the center-left, would moderate the market, while in the Soviet Union and states inspired by it, the state would simply dominate. For a time, this was the common sense of governing, pretty much everywhere (Chase-Dunn and Almeida 2020).

The neoliberal mission was to destroy this consensus, mounting ethical arguments about individual freedom and efficiency arguments about the wisdom of the market and the stupidity of the state.[41] We do not have space to review that history here, but simply posit that a new common sense took hold in the halls of power virtually worldwide, in which "less state, more market" came to be the prevailing economic nostrum, the default. The declining attractiveness of the Soviet Union as a model, meanwhile, meant that fears of Left revolution diminished in the wealthier democracies, decreasing the incentive of those in power to maintain social safety nets. The collapse of Communist rule in Europe and China's turn to authoritarian capitalism confirmed the wisdom of such currents, further eroding support for pro-labor policies.

At the same time, less affluent parts of the world experienced their own vast change in the culture of power. Key sources of international finance had been lending vast funds to poorer countries for development projects.[42] By the 1980s, the bill was coming due in Latin America and by the 1990s, in Africa. But now the banks were hostile to state-led development and keen on budget-cutting; the institutions of global finance demanded slashing public-sector employment, subsidies for services, state budgets, and tax capacity, as well as weakening labor rights and protective tariff barriers as conditions for further support. Thus, in many countries at very different places in the world economic order, there was a convergence on austerity as the solution to everything, "the medicine of choice" as Shefner and Blad (2020: 6) put it. Privatization, deregulation, and defunding public services from health to education now became the new common sense of rule.

The geographically vast wave of democratizations therefore coincided with states contracting labor rights, dismantling barriers to the untrammeled pursuit of profit, and cutting social services, with accompanying widening of the gap of rich and poor. With paid employment becoming increasingly precarious, observers of many countries began to write of a new and growing *precariat* (Milkman 2017). In moments of particular hardship, governments were inclining to cut spending, not to engage in the countercyclical targeted spending policies of the previous turn of the capitalist wheel, further driving disenchantment with democracy in practice. Looking back at our graphs, we note the turn toward anarchism in Russian in the post-Communist 1990s (Figure 3), but also the slightly earlier shifts in English, French, Italian, and Spanish (Figure 2).

When serious troubles in the US housing market triggered a cascading collapse of financial institutions, followed by massive unemployment and government revenue shortfalls around the world, governments in wealthy

---

[41] It is helpful to think about neoliberalism as a social movement (Sklair 2011; Schneirov and Schneirov 2016; Chouhy 2019).

[42] The banks were awash with the enormous earnings of oil-exporting states that followed the huge petroleum price hikes of the 1970s.

democracies responded with the current nostrum, more austerity, generating a downward spiral of business failure, unemployment, collapse of consumer spending, mortgage foreclosures, state shortfalls, and challenged financial institutions, for which the solution, still more austerity, only exacerbated the crisis. This Great Recession of 2007–2008 led to enormous job loss in Mediterranean countries and astronomical unemployment among young people. In especially hard-hit Greece and Spain, and to some extent stimulated by the pro-democracy rebellions of 2011 in Egypt, itself stimulated by a similar rebellion in Tunisia, huge movements took to the streets and public squares, with economic grievances fueling serious complaints about the state of democracy. One of the Spanish *indignados'* most repeated slogans was "they call it democracy, but it isn't." Another was "real democracy – it's time." The immediate trigger of the occupation of public squares in dozens of Spanish cities by mostly young people was the looming elections of regional and local governments and the sense of many of the (mostly) youthful protestors that both major parties were committed to the austerity policies that were depriving them of a future.

A few months later, young people borrowing and modifying the Spanish example were occupying public places in the United States, claiming to speak for the 99 percent whose needs and wishes were not served in the existing US democracy, captured in the slogan "they got bailed out, we got sold out." (And, of course, as addressed earlier, many observers noted the significant anarchist current in these movements, including the arresting phrase "we are the 99%"[43] (Roberts 2020).) The legacy of these movements of 2011 to the movements of the next decade was enormous. The huge multicountry survey of the attitudes of youth toward democracy to which we have already referred presents an extremely revealing graph of satisfaction with democracy among young people (ages 18–34) over time in the five European countries hit most hard by the crisis. In the decade preceding the Great Recession, a majority of young people expressed satisfaction. But when youth unemployment jumped, "youth assessments of democratic performance soured" (Foa et al. 2020: 18). In fact, the graph of satisfaction with democracy and the inverted graph of excess youth unemployment track each other almost perfectly.

4.2.4 Globalization

The developing web of cross-border interaction challenges the capacity of states to manage crises and also challenges citizens' confidence that state decisions

---

[43] Anarchist David Graeber (2013: 41), often credited with coining the phrase, gives his own account of its origin.

represent their voices. Consider some of the global problems confronting humanity in the twenty-first century: *global climate change and associated disasters*, something requiring concerted global action if anything ever did; *threats of economic disruption with rapid flows of investment from place to place* and the certainty that the Great Recession of 2008–2009 and the COVID-19-induced recession of 2020 will not be the last; the likelihood of *future global pandemics* and the certainly that COVID-19 is not the last new pathogen that will find mass human targets; the *propensity for globalized capitalism to develop and deploy new technologies with potentially far-reaching destructive consequences in the relentless pursuit of profits* (e.g., extracting petroleum or minerals from beneath the floor of the oceans or rapidly diffusing ever-enhanced artificial intelligence capacities); *transnationalized criminality* (as in the narcotics trade); the vast *migrations* that have already begun as climate change wipes out established livelihoods while criminal violence and war and growing impoverishment drive people to seek work and peace; and *the radical inadequacy of interstate dispute-resolution mechanisms* to prevent states with horrific weapons from using them as they wish. None of these issues can be managed by one or a small group of countries. Continuing failure by democratic states leads to growing disenchantment with democracy in those states, just as the failure of democratic states to adequately address the suffering of the economic dislocations of the twenty years after the First World War led to widespread embrace of antidemocratic politics, including fascism.

After the end of the Second World War, as the profoundly wounded European colonial powers proved unable to prevent their colonies' movements for self-rule from achieving national independence, one could have imagined that a more democratic world would mean the separate democratization of all the independent states in which now most of the human population resided, one by one. But the very success of national independence revealed a world of tightening transnational connection combined with vast differences in national wealth and power. This meant that the termination of a half-millennium of colonial expansion was also the beginning of the great disillusion with national democracy as the sole goal to which democrats should aspire. The discrediting of the states as the core institution for creating a more democratic order has had major implications for contemporary radicalism, less inclined to spend all its energies on the achievement of state power and instead oriented toward alternatives including hyperlocal and extra-governmental, directly democratic organizations and solutions.[44]

---

[44] Neighborhood-based mutual aid efforts in response to the global pandemic are examples.

Neoliberalism is a global project (Almeida and Pérez Martín 2022). The failures of neoliberal democracy have also been strengthening forces on the political Right, also a transnational phenomenon – scholars are beginning to speak of an emerging Global Right (Bob 2012; Chase-Dunn and Almeida 2020: 118–144). We cannot pursue this important subject here other than to note that it has added energy and urgency to contemporary Left radicalism, including anarchism and antifascist mobilizations. As journalists and scholars debate the usefulness of characterizing recently strengthened antidemocratic movements as "fascist," some of those frightened or disgusted by these movements embrace an antifascist label. A part of today's radicalism exhibits the movement–countermovement dynamics classically analyzed by Meyer and Staggenborg (1996), including a mutual radicalization.

Summing up this portion of our argument: By the end of the twentieth century and continuing into the twenty-first, many forces were catalyzing calls for deep change. Activists were increasingly convinced that simply availing themselves of opportunities to replace one group of incumbents of office with another is profoundly inadequate for the intersecting crises of the twenty-first century. But why has the ensuing radicalism on the Left tilted toward anarchism?

4.3 Rejecting Some Venerable Radical Paths

Activists have explicit or implicit theories of how to make a more just future that connects action in the present with their goals. When these theories are explicit, we often speak of ideologies. Our task in this and the next sections is to try to explain why in the later twentieth and early twenty-first centuries activists' practices increasingly resemble those found in the history of anarchism. The graphs of word frequencies and the tabulations of newspaper reports with which we began suggest that we might usefully think of an explanation as having two components: a turning away from activist practices associated with "socialism" and an embrace of activist practices associated with "anarchism." But we must be clear that we are explaining an overlapping shift rather than a total rejection of one thing for another, especially because the histories of anarchism and socialism are intertwined. As we have argued in the first part of this essay, our evidence shows that in the early twenty-first century, even some of those deploying the language of socialism display practices with an anarchist flavor. So we are dividing this part of our argument into accounting for a *turning from* the one and a *turning toward* the other. We dwell at length on the negative because rejection of unsatisfactory situations drives movements to create something new (Markoff et al. 2021).

The negative part of our argument is straightforward, but we will find it useful to distinguish three projects: (1) the project of "socialist revolution" in which a group that claims to be battling for a radically egalitarian and more just order seizes state power either by managing to gain control of central state institutions as the old order disintegrates (let us call this the Bolshevik model) or because it has organized a (usually) protracted armed struggle, defeated the armed forces of the old regime, and now occupies the centers of state power – call this the *guerrilla* model; (2) the project of "democratic socialism" – achieving power within a constitutional democracy primarily by legal electoral contestation and social movement activism, using the power of the state they challenge to bring about transformative change; and (3) the "anarchist project" of building the new within the shell of the old while autonomously attacking the organs of systemic domination where possible.[45] We advance a simple, negative contention. Both the revolutionary seizure of state power and the attainment of democratic socialism through the ballot box have disappointed and seem increasingly unpromising to radical activists.

4.4 The Socialist Revolution Project

The costs have often been enormous and the achievements toward an emancipatory, egalitarian, and democratic order have been limited. Breaking a lot of eggs yielded little in omelets. The vast killing under Stalin was followed by the vast, and for a while concealed, killing under Mao, and many other forms of repression as well. The defeat of first the French and then the Americans by determined socialist revolutionaries in what used to be called Indochina was followed by the Khmer Rouge's auto-genocide in Cambodia, Vietnam's invasion of Cambodia and China's of Vietnam (rupturing any notion of socialist solidarity), and hundreds of thousands of fleeing Vietnamese boat people. There was, and is, the ongoing repression in North Korea. Some might have imagined at points in the past that such violence was the painful birth pangs of the new order, but post-Stalinist bureaucratic ossification was not the new order toward which democratic revolutionaries aspired either. These upheavals were all certainly transformative, but the results were usually new kinds of oppressive states, not an end to oppression.

---

[45] We found very stimulating the deep analysis of imagined paths to deep social transformation of Erik Olin Wright (2010) but have modified his three-part classification in developing our own. Our "democratic socialism project" does not distinguish Wright's "ruptural" electoral success from his piece-by-piece accumulation of smaller symbiotic advances through the ballot box. As it happened empirically, or rather as it did not happen, neither electoral strategy ever resulted in superseding capitalism anywhere; we simply group these two together as "democratic socialism." Our "anarchist project" fits within Wright's "interstitial" strategy.

Even for those who are still tempted to replicate the seizure of power in a moment of state collapse, as in 1917, or the organization of revolutionary guerrilla warfare, democratic states have proved very poor launching points for such revolutionary projects. We will not attempt an analysis here of why they have not been – just an empirical question: when the starting point is liberal democracy, which is then brought to an end, how often have the subsequent occupants of the halls of power been socialist revolutionaries? Three empirical generalizations: First, when something reasonably called parliamentary democracy has collapsed, as in interwar twentieth-century Europe, the Right was the usual victor, even when the Left was part of destabilizing the previous democratic system.

Second, actually pulling off a revolutionary conquest of the state has increasingly proved elusive. In the wake of Cuba's revolution, an inspirational model for radicals in other places, many attempted to wage guerrilla war in Latin America, but only in Nicaragua was there success, and that success lasted but a few years.[46] In rich countries, this became an utterly unpromising path. Przeworski et al. (2000) showed that no democratic regime with a per capita income higher than that of Argentina in 1975 was ever overthrown, a statement amended by Przeworski two decades later (2019: 33) to encompass the slightly higher per capita income of Thailand in 2006, when the Thai army overthrew the elected government. The scarcity of victories for the revolutionary Left when democracies collapse and the (thus far) absence of democratic collapse for countries at the level of national incomes of the wealthy democracies of the twenty-first century have drastically decreased the attractiveness of these strategies – even without taking into consideration the unhappy, and often disastrous, results of success. The obvious rejoinder is that foes of liberal democracy may think up new ways to end it, making statements generalizing from past practice irrelevant in the future.[47]

Third, the urbanizing populations and the ever-shrinking weight of rural production in national economies have made successful pursuit of rural guerrilla struggles less promising than at earlier points, in poorer as well as richer countries. At the same time, increases in state surveillance and weapons

---

[46] And the return of Daniel Ortega to power at the ballot box in 2007 launched a new authoritarian regime to boot.

[47] Since the failed US coup in the first days of 2021, those determined to end established democracy in that country have included the previous president, a majority of the members of one of the two major parties in the House of Representatives, numerous armed groups, and a large portion of the electorate. Like other movements, they may learn from failure how to do better in the future. If they succeed, Przeworski's past-based empirical generalization about high national incomes effectively warding off democratic collapse will need further amending. Perhaps the recent evisceration of democracy in Hungary suggests that it already needs amending.

technology has given armed struggles from below waning chances for survival, never mind offensive success. So, in the latter half of the twentieth century, those seeking radical transformations were simply less and less inclined to follow this path as the unhappy news of the results of successful conquest of power and of failures to even conquer power continued to mount.[48] That is why some scholars have been wondering if revolution can be reconceived for the twenty-first century (Foran 2003; Smith et al. 2017), shifting the focus away from "common associations of revolution with the militant takeover of the state" (Smith et al. 2017: 236).[49]

4.5 The Democratic Socialism Project

From the nineteenth century, parts of the socialist movement sought state control not through insurrection or guerrilla warfare but through the ballot box. The failure to move beyond capitalism by use of the institutional and legal mechanisms provided by democratic states has been very well analyzed (e.g., by Wright 2010: 308–320 and 337–365; Przeworski and Sprague 1986; Eley 2002). There are mutually reinforcing barriers that have blocked this hopeful path out of capitalism, consequences of the *logic of democratic electoral competition*, the *logic of democratic governance*, the *logic of states in the global order of states,* and the contradictory *logic of formal citizen equality with significant disparities in citizen economic power.*

4.5.1 Electoral Issues

Since the industrial proletariat has practically never constituted an electoral majority, Socialist parties have had to broaden their appeals beyond this group, thereby diluting their ideological commitments and weakening a worker identity among their adherents. And since, at least in the short run, the potential economic disruption of a transition to socialism would diminish worker well-being, even if there are compelling future benefits, workers who would bear the costs of transition have often been leery of socialist radicalism and favor "moderation." In addition, workers are not only workers but have many social identities that might influence their vote – religious, ethnic, political, and so forth (Przeworski and Sprague 1986).

---

[48] According to data comparing public, civilian, mass mobilizations to overthrow regimes with waging warfare to overthrow them, Chenoweth and Stephan's data (2011: 8) show a pronounced decline in revolutionary warfare as a strategy for change.

[49] Unpublished research of Case and Lazar shows some identification with Stalinism or Maoism among recent US activists but not weakening the generally anarchist culture.

4.5.2 Governance Issues

As representatives of a working class, a Socialist party entering government will generally have to govern in coalition with other parties, setting a brake on what can be achieved at the ballot box. This is clearest for parliamentary systems, but even in a presidential system like the United States, victorious parties often have had to seek support from rival party members in order to pass legislation. Moreover, the culture of governing distances parliamentary representatives and socialist officials from the citizens who voted for them, making socialists in power increasingly like the officialdom of other parties. By the early twentieth century, this trend was classically and brilliantly analyzed with reference to the world's most noted Socialist party, the German SPD, by Robert Michels (1962 [1911]). In addition, the limited capacity of democratically elected parliaments to actually control the growing executive bureaucracies, which had a logic of their own, further limited the likelihood of an electoral path to socialism, as analyzed by Max Weber (1968, v. 3: 1410–1419). These trends have been convincingly substantiated by the fates of Pink Tide governments in Latin America in the twenty-first century where bureaucratic tendencies in Venezuela and Bolivia, for instance, undercut promising attempts for transitions to socialism (Fernandes 2010; Oikonamakis and Espinoza 2014).

4.5.3 World-Systemic Issues

As one state in a system of states, and with the end of formal colonial rule by the late twentieth century, the mimetic pressures of other states have acted as a great constraint on state forms and practices. Such processes have been analyzed in detail by Meyer et al. (2009). No one has more forcefully insisted on understanding states not as separate entities but as part of a system of states and as structures in a global capitalist world-system than Immanuel Wallerstein and his associates (2004). After the Second World War, beyond the general pressures of the state system, there were specific pressures from the hegemonic capitalist state at that point, the United States, whose political order, uniquely among the wealthy democratic states, lacked any strong Socialist party and which was especially hostile to any socialist leanings among its democratic allies, let alone any socialist dangers anywhere else (Sassoon 1996: 112 has a fine formulation of this point). Some would argue that in the twenty-first century, states themselves have become subordinated to the logic of global capitalist accumulation – above and beyond the influence of a hegemonic state such as the USA – a trend that was particularly clear in Latin America (Robinson 2008).

4.5.4 Inequality Issues

In the middle of the nineteenth century, Marx argued that liberal democracy embodied a fundamental contradiction, its combination of formal equality before the law with class-based disparities of economic resources. Poorer citizens might eventually achieve formally equal voting rights (and were far from having done so when Marx began to analyze this problem), but in class-stratified societies would have less capacity to hire lawyers, publicists, or campaign staff workers; they would also have less capacity to lobby elected representatives or influence state bureaucrats. Those with economic power would increase their political power, used in turn to defend or increase their wealth, and so on. The extreme and growing inequalities of the US since the later twentieth century, to take a notorious example, means that the astronomical sums increasingly necessary to mount political campaigns, with few and weakly enforced limits on campaign spending, make elections into vast occasions for legalized bribery.[50]

With four such powerful sources of constraint, small wonder that although nominally Socialist parties have sometimes held a share of power in democratic states, socialism has not been achieved through this route, not ever, precisely as was predicted by Michels (and by anarchists' analyses [e.g., Kropotkin 1892]). Such parties, however, have sometimes played a key role in enacting many extremely significant reform measures, reshaping capitalism and greatly improving workers' lives, but they have not transcended capitalism, not even remotely. They have been major forces for institutionalizing and expanding the meanings of democracy, but they have never brought about socialism.[51]

In recent decades, moreover, such Left parties have become permeated by the neoliberal project. Stephanie Mudge (2018) has argued that these parties have been, in fact, major impellers of neoliberalism within the wealthy democracies. Exploring the history of parliamentary Left parties, she shows two major shifts. In Mudge's analysis, in the late nineteenth and early twentieth centuries, these parties were characterized by what she calls a "socialist leftism" that aimed at state conquest through democratic elections led by parties claiming to champion

---

[50] The contradiction of formal political equality and class inequality remains as alive as when Marx analyzed it as shown by Democratic Socialists of America republishing in 2021 an essay on this theme that Michael Harrington (2021) had first published forty years earlier. This contradiction has been, and remains, a major source of movements challenging existing democracy in the name of a future democracy (Markoff 2011).

[51] In the Global South, countries where an electoral victory seemed to offer a path to socialism either swiftly fell to military coups supported by the USA, such as in Guatemala in 1954, Republic of the Congo in 1960, and Chile in 1973, or saw democratic promises abandoned due to destabilization campaigns by the USA, verticalist logics internal to the parties, and the constraints of global capitalism, as in Venezuela under Chavez and Bolivia under Evo Morales.

the modern working class. This was superseded by an "economistic leftism" in which this unachieved revolutionary objective was replaced by policies aimed at taming the market through the sorts of economic policies now summed up as "Keynesian" and thereby reducing the sufferings of vulnerable workers, and poorer people generally, through the establishment of social safety nets, especially in the wake of the disasters of the Second World War and guided by economists with Left sympathies.

Successful reform in one country encouraged reforms in others. But in a second shift, in place by the 1990s, these parties assumed a pro-business stance, arguing that it was capitalist profits that fueled job-creating investments, that deregulation and budget-cutting would encourage economic growth whose benefits would ultimately accrue to workers and the poor, and that reforming welfare systems to tie benefits to incentives to work would more effectively alleviate poverty and be a lot less expensive for middle-class taxpayers. The successful proponents of this new "neoliberal Left" held themselves to be realists, embracing the claim of Britain's Margaret Thatcher on the right that there was "no alternative." Mudge's point is that neoliberalism is not only a body of ideas and policies promoted by the political Right but over the decades came to dominate the parliamentary Left as well, at least in the rich countries she examined. The mainstream Left moved toward neoliberalism and was important in enacting its policies; the mainstream Right had been there already and only got a little bit more so. Mudge's analysis suggests that the usual Anglo-American icons of neoliberalism, Tory Thatcher and Republican Reagan, might well be replaced by Labourite Blair and Democrat Clinton.

Was something similar happening in the parliamentary Left in other places? Gabriel Chouhy (2022) has studied party programs in post-military Chile and Uruguay and finds "the trend in both countries is consistent with the general neoliberal shift in Western democracies" and that "even when the Center-Left was in power, government platforms included significant neoliberal elements." Although the data does show some decline in neoliberalism during the Pink Tide for which Latin America is noted, the bigger story is neoliberalism's ascent. In further work, Chouhy has found a similar pattern for Brazil, Argentina, and perhaps Bolivia as well.[52]

4.6 Transformational Change in the Twenty-First Century

There are several other significant ways twenty-first century radicalisms depart from previous radical traditions. Many past analyses presume there is a single or central axis of inequality, generally identified with social class, and developed strategies to bring working-class-based socialism to power within individual states,

---

[52] We thank Chouhy for sharing his unpublished graphs.

but often neglected the pressures states exert on one another in a global system.[53] We can briefly point to aspects of contemporary radicalism that in important ways move beyond these mostly implicit presuppositions. Each of these points deserves, and has often received, extended analysis. Here we will simply summarize.

4.6.1 Multiple Forms of Oppression

Many twenty-first century activists do not accept that economic class struggle, important as it has been, is the master key to overcoming injustice and oppression. They participate in movements concerned with racism, decolonization, environmental injustices, commodification, policing of sexuality and gender, indigeneity, and much more, without necessarily agreeing on how or if each of these may be related to class war. Eley's (2002) history of the European Left shows convincingly how the emergence of the New Left in the 1960s and beyond was greeted with mockery, fury, and fear by the Socialist and Communist parties of the time precisely because of its embrace of such concerns. The hostility of the established Socialist parties only deepened the search for new directions by the young radicals. Eley argues that the rigidity of those established parties in fact accounts in considerable part for their decline. Much early twenty-first century radicalism, in its embrace of intersectional visions, is carrying forward these New Left challenges of a half-century before. Note that Figures 2 and 3 show the shift toward anarchism coinciding with the New Left.

4.6.2 Transnational Activism

Many twenty-first century activists are persuaded that the separate national states are not the only vehicles for social transformation, and many are doubtful that they are the principal ones. Activists across the world increasingly identify their local conditions with global crises and understand that these are not separately manageable by national states. Much activism now coordinates across national borders and targets the institutions of transnational decision-making (Smith 2008; Smith and Wiest 2012). The national state, whose conquest was seen as the key to a socialist transformation from the mid-nineteenth century on, is no longer the presumed goal of activist strategy (see also Chase-Dunn and Almeida 2020). Note that Tables 1 and 2 show an acceleration of earlier anarchist trends in the twenty-first century.[54]

---

[53] A fine example is Wright's (2010) analysis, on which we have built.

[54] Activists committed to solidarity across national boundaries and to anarchist practice may confront a tension between favoring consensus decision-making and nationally distinctive activist cultures (Flesher Fominaya 2014).

4.6.3 Local Activism

As activists' understanding of problems is increasingly global, immediate goals are often in local arenas, working within and between communities around immediate concerns. As local activists coordinate with each other, or learn from each other, the new local activism sometimes becomes what is being called translocal activism (e.g., by Schroering 2021). For such purposes, big, centralized, national parties seem largely irrelevant as networks of locally knowledgeable and locally engaged activists develop their agendas, strategies, and actions (Manski and Smith 2019).

4.7 Conclusion on Failed Transformative Strategies

The revolutionary conquest of power by seizing the state through planned insurrection or protracted warfare has had catastrophic human costs and has not so far led to generalized emancipation even when successful revolutionary parties have remained in charge across decades. In the twenty-first century, these strategies are even less likely to liberate the world.

The democratic conquest of power through electoral means has at times achieved important reforms but has increasingly backed far away from the sorts of transformation that would move beyond capitalism. Instead, democratic parties commonly described as left-of-center have become part of the fabric of neoliberal capitalism, and played a major role in dismantling some of the worker protections these same parties' earlier reforms had done so much to propel forward.

Movements formed around the advance of worker rights from the nineteenth century on have played pivotal roles in democratizing some states and in enlarging the meanings of democracy, but they have not achieved socialism and have often been inadequate in speaking to many other human concerns and experiences of injustice. New movements raising these grievances in the 1960s separated themselves from the established Lefts of their day. Many twenty-first century activists have what is commonly known as an intersectional perspective (see Crenshaw 1989; Collins 2019). Unlike the 1960s, however, this view is becoming dominant.

To many twenty-first century movements, conquest of state apparatuses is no longer the pivotal goal from which all else follows; some are abandoning it, while others understand the need to join national state politics to both local and transnational strategies.

4.8 Saying Yes to Anarchism

Disinclined to pursue much-trodden paths, twenty-first century radicals are looking elsewhere. They are less preoccupied by the seizure of state power, whether by arms or votes; less convinced that there is a single axis of oppression; and less inclined to subordinate the goal of democracy within a movement in order to advance their power within the state. And they are more inclined to withdraw from or confront the state; develop forms of mutual aid; see struggles for justice as eternally ongoing rather than pursue a final victory; and take satisfaction in local action interconnected through radical values rather than follow party lines. Put this way, it should be unsurprising that visions for a better world, how to work together to bring that about, and what sorts of actions make sense to do so are being lifted from an anarchist playbook. Many twenty-first century activists are attracted by movement organizations that grapple with making democracy and participatory politics within as well as beyond that organization, that embrace mutual aid projects, and that work for change locally as a down payment on systemic change. Whether or not they are studying anarchism's history or reading its theorists, whether they apply the label or not, they are pursuing anarchist practices.

4.8.1 Anti-capitalism

Anarchism provided activists with a viable radical critique of capitalism – and the neoliberalism of recent decades, in particular – without the baggage attached to Soviet authoritarianism or Socialist parties that have long since given up on socialism in practice. "Anarchists are wholeheartedly anti-capitalist and consider the state inseparable from the capitalist system," explains Angela Wigger in her discussion of an anarchist political economy. Furthermore, "[t]he capitalist state is criticized for codifying, legitimizing and representing social inequalities through a hierarchical and authoritarian concentration of power in the hands of ruling classes" (Wigger 2014: 741).

4.8.2 Horizontalism and Direct Democracy

Anarchism's call for decentralization of power through horizontal models and directly democratic practices specifically addresses the concerns held by many activists about corporate globalization, while welcoming connections across national borders, including among anti-capitalist activists. Modeling alternative social and organizational forms that diffused the locus of power from capitalist hegemons to people acting collectively had broad appeal for anti-capitalists arguing that democracy needed to be reimagined, including democracy within activist decision-making. The Zapatistas were influential because they manifested an inspiring model of opposition and alternatives to neoliberal policies. The mass events like the protests in Seattle and Prague that followed added a sense of momentum, as growing emphasis on horizontal structures and direct democracy spoke to the widespread failings of national democracy in the neoliberal era.

4.8.3 Direct Action

Among the Left at the turn of the twenty-first century, there was a transnationally shared sense of urgency as well as a desire for more immediate changes that could be achieved without a revolutionary party or vanguard. A potent combination of rage at failed systems and states was joined with a more hopeful, utopian desire to demonstrate that "another world is possible" (Solnit 2004; Graeber 2008; Thompson 2010; Manski et al. 2020). The anarchist emphasis on direct action allowed for a collective expression that was a source of empowerment for those looking to prove that there was "power in the people."

There is an important distinction between much "civil disobedience" and anarchist versions of "direct action." Civil disobedience and direct action sometimes have similar tactical repertoires, but they are embedded in different strategic visions of how to advance toward deep social transformation. The purpose of civil disobedience – publicly breaking laws one considers to be unjust – is generally to compel authorities to change their behavior. The purpose of direct action is to reduce or remove the role of authorities. This is a difference that often remains invisible to studies of movement activism that limit themselves to cataloging the forms of action because it requires understanding of activist purpose. Direct action aims to act autonomously "as if one is already free ... Insofar as one is capable, one proceeds as if the state does not exist" (Graeber 2013). So, while activists engaging in civil disobedience may strive to pressure the state to adopt some sort of reform, the direct actionist sets out not only to disrupt business as usual but also to discover what it would look like to be free from state domination. For anarchists, direct action is the "rejection of participation in parliamentary or statist politics and the adoption of tactics and strategies which ... [are] about empowering [people] and breaking the dependency on others" (Brannigan 2005). And while anarchism is not the only radical current to embrace direct action, anarchists not only imbue it with this revolutionary intent but are especially associated with it, and known for their willingness to take immediate, sometimes militant, action.

4.8.4 Prefigurative Politics

Anarchism offers a chance for those seeking a new world to begin remaking the social order themselves, right away. According to one veteran Global Justice anarchist organizer based in DC, prefigurative politics means to "embody the ideas and the ethics that you're advocating for in the work that you're doing" such as putting horizontalism and directly democratic consensus decision-making into practice.[55] Contemporary expressions of this, influenced by the prefigurative

---

[55] Unpublished interview by Hillary Lazar, February 2017.

practices of the New Left and feminist movements and most closely by social anarchism and mobilizations such as the GJM and Occupy, mean to undo all forms of oppression and domination, including forms of domination within the movement itself. Perhaps one of the most obvious examples of prefigurative politics is mutual aid, which directly speaks to widespread perception of state failure. When the state no longer provides for us in times of crisis, people turn to each other. Prefigurative politics addressed twenty-first century Leftists' desire for rapid and tangible social transformation.

4.8.5 Intersections

Finally, anarchism is distinct from much of the history of socialism in the emphasis it places on eliminating *all* forms of hierarchy and domination. Anarchists have hardly been alone in challenging neoliberalism, but the openness of anarchist politics to intersectional analyses of multiple axes of oppression distinguishes it, for example, from those strategies for which class struggle was so dominant that other issues were to be postponed and their advocates consigned to auxiliary sub-movements.[56] As one long-term anarchist organizer active in Global Justice, climate justice, and mutual aid efforts, expresses it: "intersectionality of movements and communities is not abstract . . . the choices we have made about the environment, economy, race . . . they are all interconnected and cannot be separated."[57] This has made anarchism more resonant with other radical currents that have grown in prominence such as Black feminism, queer liberation, and decolonial thought – in no small part through the critical interventions of Black, queer, feminist, indigenous, and other activists of color into contemporary Left activism as well as anarchist theory and practice (Lazar 2018). The strong presence of anarchists in the GJM (evident in the research of Chase-Dunn and Almeida 2020) also connected anarchists with these other currents (Lazar 2018).

4.9 Horizontalism, Technology, and Transnational Connections

Since the late twentieth century, activists have had new tools for exploring interstitial and alternative strategies, most prominently digital communication technologies. These technologies have enabled expansive possibilities for communication and collaboration across, as well as within, borders, facilitating the spread of ideas and activist-to-activist connections across geographies, movements, and social backgrounds. In so doing, they have empowered

---

[56] The centrality of the male worker to much of the history of the European Left is marvelously analyzed by Eley (2002) as is the significance of the movements of the later twentieth century that challenged that centrality.

[57] Unpublished interview by Hillary Lazar, June 2021.

individual and collective resistance to established authority and given authorities new tools to monitor dissent.[58]

In enabling ready person-to-person communication across boundaries of
organizations, national states, and movements, the new communicative
technologies support translocal and transnational organizing, facilitate
change in interorganizational alliances, and enable horizontalism, all con-
gruent with anarchist strategies. By empowering all with access to the
Internet via phones and computers to connect, they suit those suspicious
of controlling leaderships and unquestioned, all-embracing ideologies. By
enabling mobilizations without elaborate and expensive organization, they
enable sudden seizures of opportunity, including by marginalized voices
(although they may also be enabling mobilizations without organizational
follow-up and exclusion of the many in the world without technological
access). All these fit with anarchist practice.[59] The state's enhanced capacity
for surveillance also supercharges its repressive capabilities, but at the same
time, open-source encryption technologies that allow activists to leak government and corporate documents and to shield their communications from
authorities can engender mass capacity and the will to resist (Case and
Stribling-Uss 2023).

But we wonder whether the greatest impact on activism may be cultural
and longer-term. Although the Internet originated in a project of the US
defense establishment, it soon developed a decentralized, multi-origin, self-
organizing style of growth, resembling in its remarkable evolution more the
dreams of anarchists than generals (Markoff 2001) and has, thus far, been
resistant to efforts by fearful governments or avaricious corporations to
acquire control, although some governments have been able to monitor it,
restrict access, modify its workings, or intermittently shut it down, and some
huge corporations have made vast fortunes from its new resources. Consider
as well the everyday use of Wikipedia, whose organizing principles are
characterized by Wright (2010: 194–203; quotes from 195 and 199) as
"not simply *non*-capitalist; they are thoroughly *anti*-capitalist" (195)
because they embody "non-market relations, egalitarian participation,
deliberative interactions among contributors, democratic governance and
adjudication," which "conform closely to the normative ideals of radical
democratic egalitarianism" that have involved "tens of thousands of people
across the world in the *production* of a massive global resource."[60]

---

[58] This borrows from Burridge and Markoff (2023).

[59] Chase-Dunn and Almeida (2020: 83–84) provide quantitative evidence that transnational activism is greatly facilitated by well-developed Internet infrastructure.

[60] Wikipedia as a self-organized community: Konieczny (2009, 2017).

For young people, growing up with the new devices and connectivity a taken-for-granted piece of reality, imagining a capacity for human self-organization without coercive hierarchy may be simply easier than for generations past. With such a part of the taken-for-granted everyday, anarchist dreams and anarchist organization seem less far-fetched.

4.10 Building on a Legacy

At many points in our argument, we have seen that recent practices have drawn on those developed a half-century earlier in the New Left. This not-so-distant experience of challenging Socialist orthodoxy was there to build on, when the mounting problems of the late twentieth century called forth a new hunger for radical transformation and brought the experience of older activists into contact with the young. We have tried to demonstrate, and explain, this latest anarchist turn, but there is also a story of recurrence. Our graphs and tables show this to be the third major transnational anarchist surge since the modern origins of anarchism as a social movement. While we have not attempted to explain these earlier surges here, we have often in our text referred to the legacies of this past as it has been drawn on by this latest burst, situating the anarchist turn in the long and ongoing history of revolutionary struggle from the Left.[61]

4.11 The Anarchist Spirit and the Urgency of the Times

While much of this anarchist story centers on popular dissatisfaction with palpably failing political and economic systems, these same circumstances also fuel ethnocentric nationalisms, xenophobia, racism, violent enforcement of gender and sexual normativity, and interstate warfare. "Fascism" has returned to the vocabulary of political analysis and debate. A sense of acute urgency grows from the magnitude of onrushing problems, including evident multispecies extinctions, powerhouse storms, drought-induced fires, and relentless rise in sea levels, compounded by growing rightwing currents that promise to usher in political, cultural, and climate catastrophes on a global scale. Fears of this new transnationally connected Far Right, and anarchists' willingness to confront it head-on, has lent further energies to the radical currents we have described here (Bray 2017; Chase-Dunn and Almeida 2020; Burley 2022).

---

[61] We have not engaged here with continuities and discontinuities between surges in anarchist history and leave for another discussion the extent to which nineteenth-century Russian anarchists who burned to "smash the state," twentieth-century Burmese rural people who evade state attention (Scott 2009), and twenty-first-century anarchists who are trying to bring about change despite the state have a common project. Nor have we addressed the long history of human groups organizing themselves collectively without coercion, fundamental to the thinking of Kropotkin (2005 [1902]) and recently highlighted by Bamyeh (2010).

Anarchism, or at the very least anarchist principles and praxis, speak to the concerns of the age without the baggage of discredited alternatives. And its growth in the twenty-first century reflects a confluence of the compelling revolutionary possibilities that it offers, along with its popularization and global diffusion first during the GJM, in the revolutionary upsurges of 2011, and by the latent anarchist spirit that has existed among all peoples throughout history that is moving to the fore amidst today's crises.

5 Conclusion: Black is the New Red

"It is becoming increasingly clear that the age of revolutions is not over. It's becoming equally clear that the global revolutionary movement in the twenty first century, will be one that traces its origins less to the tradition of Marxism, or even of socialism narrowly defined, but of anarchism" (Graeber and Grubačić 2004).

We started thinking about this essay in 2019, just before COVID-19 claimed so many lives and upended so many plans. In 2020 and continuing into the next years, the multiple crises impelled by a viral pathogen were providing further evidence of the humanly inadequate character of the social and political order – and of the diffusion of anarchist modes of pushback. Now, in 2023, it seems a safe bet that the forces generating today's radicalism will continue to do so for some time to come and that many of these radicals will be borrowing from an anarchist playbook.

As we are concluding our study in late Spring 2023, barricades are burning in multiple countries. Among these, everyday Iranians are leading a historic uprising against violent patriarchy and political–religious orthodoxy. The uprising was triggered by the "Morality Police" arresting, beating, and killing an Iranian Kurdish woman, Jina (or Mahsa) Amini, for not sufficiently covering her head in public (though this dress code violation is not obvious in the video that soon circulated). Once again, no party or formal organization started the protests nor has one emerged from them, and no overall leaders have emerged – or been called for. The resonant slogan of the movement, "woman life freedom," comes from Turkey's Kurdish minority. Picked up by the Syrian Kurds of Rojava, whose anarchist dimensions (including the ideological influence of a prominent anarchist theorist) are evident, it then passed to Iran's Kurds and then, following the police murder, to Iranian protestors generally, who gave it to the rest of us (Filiu 2022; Afary and Anderson 2022).[62]

Not far away, protests are rocking Israel, Iran's bitter political rival, in the largest internal uprising of its citizens in that country's history. Facing growing

---

[62] "Resonant": Inspired by the protests, Shervin Hajipour's song "For" won a Grammy in 2023 (www.youtube.com/c/Shervinine).

mobilizations across society protesting authoritarian moves by the government of Benjamin Netanyahu, the prime minister began referring to protesters by the worst epithet he could muster: *anarchists*.[63] Indeed, just as anarchist practices are moving to the fore of resistance struggles, anarchists are once again drawing the focus of security forces and agents of the status quo. The month we completed this Element, the cover of *The Atlantic* displayed a masked protester returning a tear gas cannister to police. The story proclaimed, "The New Anarchy: America faces a type of extremist violence it does not know how to stop." Written by the magazine's Executive Editor, the article breathlessly sounds the alarm at the anarchist domestic terrorist threat, a peril to liberal democracy as great as danger posed by fascists, decrying anarchists who physically confront fascists in the streets as "radicals ... without restraint, or in many cases, humanity" (LaFrance 2023: 24).

As we have shown, popular attention to *anarchism* has risen sharply in comparison to other Left ideologies. Many leftist groups self-identify as anarchist and authorities are demonizing anarchists as the spreaders of chaos and disorder. But the influence of anarchist ideas runs far deeper than even the label itself; the standard by which the Left organizes itself today has become anarchist.

We have argued that anarchist practices have become attractive alternatives to those seeking radical change who are unattracted by other historically important strategic options. To the failures of national democracy, twenty-first century radicalism proposes strengthening participatory democracy. To the failures of capitalism, it proposes federated worker-controlled economies. To the failures of electoral politics, it proposes community-based decision-making grounded in direct action and mutual aid. To the mirage of technocratic solutions, it directs attention to human relations and acting in the here and now. To the violent threat of racism, today's activists echo the Zapatistas in proclaiming: one world in which many worlds fit. New communications technologies not only enable ready sharing of experience across national borders but also make horizontal connection and grassroots collective organization and initiative a part of the daily experience of younger activists. A new kind of radical vision is growing in the practices of generations of activists, rooted in diverse, local, national, and global struggles, learning from each other, and with a sense of growing urgency.

By the 1970s, direct colonial rule had been brought to an end but not huge wealth and power differences between and within states, nor the capital-driven

---

[63] See Maltz 2023. This *Haaretz* article does a poor job of explicating anarchism but accurately reports Netanyahu's use of the term.

world-system that governs this vast inequality. By the 1980s, a bureaucratically ossified Soviet regime no longer inspired, and beyond 1989, the champions of neoliberalism were barely slowed by fears of working-class militancy and revolution. The ensuing combination of widespread, national-level democracy and neoliberal capitalism exacerbated discontents with both. Increasingly, energized radical activists, sometimes inspired by the activists of the 1960s and subsequent decades, unenthusiastic about many venerable leftist strategies but seeking deep change, adopted what we have been calling anarchist practices, often without that label. Capitalism carried on its centuries-old capacity to generate major crises, and we have especially noted the role of the financial crisis of 2008–2009 in stimulating rage about prevailing economic and political order, intensified in the following decade with the strengthening of the Global Right and worsening of conditions for millions injured by climate crises and state failure during the pandemic of 2020. By the beginning of the twenty-first century's third decade, anarchism and anarchists – whether explicit or implicit, big-A or small-a – were culturally salient in languages spoken by billions of people and were being demonized and defended in major newspapers. Even some organizations that bore a socialist label were part of this trend. Since the turn of the millennium, the Red Threat of the Left is hoisting the black flag of anarchism.

Afterword: A Brief Note on Lessons for the Study of Contentious Politics

Some of the observations we have offered here are not new, building on work by others, but now with the helpful vantage point of writing three decades into the millennium and the benefit of being able to muster a broad range of data, regional expertise, and personal ties to some of these movements through this collaborative (dare we say, horizontally conducted) project. This is just a starting point for further conversations. We have shown an increase in both explicit and implicit anarchism, but that raises the question of further exploring the relationship between them. To what extent, for example, have explicit anarchists carried anarchism into non-anarchist mobilizations, so that we may speak of diffusion processes? And to what extent are anarchist practices emerging separately in many places in response to the many crises of the age, including within movement organizations? And questions of structural constraint and cultural toolkits also emerge: to what extent is the turn toward anarchist practice driven by pressures and possibilities that are external to the movements in which activists participate and to what extent are they impelled by a cultural transformation within activism forged by activists working together toward a common project?

Finally, there seem to be two big lessons for scholars here. *First*, we think that scholars have often neglected activists' vision of the world they hope to bring about by reducing their vision to tactical "framing"; we need to think beyond framing, valuable as that lens has been. The actions of early twenty-first century radicals, their modes of organization, and their dreams of a better future are all enmeshed with each other and need to be treated together. We could summarize this lesson as the need to pay serious attention to expressed ideology *and* the ideological orientations expressed through popular organizing models as they are occurring, not as they are imagined from afar in models designed for previous eras. As evident in the many expressions of implicit or small-a anarchism, we need to think more deeply about what actions can sometimes say even more than words or labels.

Second, we think analyses of social movements have not drawn nearly enough on theories of social change contributed by anarchists, a lacuna shared with Sociology and nearby fields generally. By the late twentieth century, an education in Sociology and nearby fields was likely to have involved the study of Marx and of Marxism, but a great deal less likely to have devoted nearly as much time to the study of any anarchist thinker, or of anarchism. There is a long history of anarchist marginalization within the Left. We could begin with Marx's theoretical battles with Proudhon, continue with his long organizational struggle with Bakunin, ponder the crushing of organized anarchism by Socialists from early in the Russian Revolution through the Spanish Revolution, and study the excoriation of the New Left, including its anarchist components, by the Communist and Socialist parties of that time. What we have shown in this study is that in our global moment of compounding crises, many activists on the Left embrace the anarchist label and even more are engaged in the kinds of practices anarchists have long championed. As social movement researchers, like other practitioners of social science, try to hear voices we have insufficiently attended to (from marginalized groups, from the Global South), we also need to hear from marginalized radical traditions, not just as objects of study but as sources of theory. This is especially the case nowadays, as so many important social movements draw from anarchism and anarchists. They have become de-marginalized as actors; we need to take them equally seriously as analysts who offer important and relevant empirical observations, theoretical interventions, social critiques, visionary reimaginings of what the world could and should be, and ideas worth grappling with about how to head there.

References

Abbas, T. and Yigit, I. H. 2015. Scenes from Gezi Park: Localisation, nationalism and globalisation in Turkey. *City: Analysis of Urban Trends, Culture, Theory, Policy, Action* 19(1), 61–76.

Abellán, J., Sequera, J., and Janoschka, M. 2012. Occupying the #Hotelmadrid: A laboratory for urban resistance. *Social Movement Studies* 11(3–4), 320–326.

Aberg-Riger, A. 2020. "Solidarity, not charity": A visual history of mutual aid. Bloomberg News: CityLab, December 22, 2020. www.bloomberg.com/news/features/2020–12-22/a-visual-history-of-mutual-aid.

Adams, M. and Lennon, M. J. 1992. Canadians, too, fault their political institutions and leaders. *Public Perspective* 3, 19–21.

Afary, J. and Anderson, K. B. 2022. Woman, life, freedom. The origins of the uprising in Iran. *Dissent*. Winter. www.dissentmagazine.org/online_articles/women-life-freedom-iran-uprising-origins. Accessed March 6, 2023.

Ainger, K. 2002. Mujeres Creando: Bolivian anarcha-feminist street activists. In Dark Star Collective, ed., *Quiet Rumors: An Anarcha-Feminist Reader*. Oakland: AK Press, 2012.

Akuno, K. and Meyer, M. 2023. *Jackson Rising Redux: Lessons on Building the Future in the Present*. Oakland: PM Press.

Almeida, P. D. 2014. *Mobilizing Democracy: Globalization and Citizen Protest*. Baltimore: Johns Hopkins University Press.

Almeida, P. D. and Pérez Martín, A. 2022. *Collective Resistance to Neoliberalism*. Cambridge: Cambridge University Press.

Anderson, W. and Samudzi, Z. 2017. The anarchism of blackness. *ROAR* 5, 70–81.

Anonymous. 2019. Lasers in the tear gas: A guide to tactics in Hong Kong. *It's Going Down*. August 13. https://itsgoingdown.org/lasers-in-the-tear-gas/. Accessed November 11, 2023.

Apoifis, N. 2016. *Anarchy in Athens: An Ethnography of Militancy, Emotions and Violence*. Manchester: Manchester University Press.

Arab Barometer. 2019. *Tunisia Country Report*. www.arabbarometer.org/wp-content/uploads/ABV_Tunisia_Report_Public-Opinion_2018-2019.pdf. Accessed November 12, 2023.

Auyero, J. 2003. *Contentious Lives: Two Argentine Women, Two Protests, and the Quest for Recognition*. Durham: Duke University Press.

Bamyeh, M. 2010. *Anarchy as Order: The History and Future of Civic Humanity*. Lanham, MD: Rowman and Littlefield.

Bamyeh, M. 2013. Anarchist method, liberal intention, authoritarian lesson: The Arab Spring between three enlightenments. *Constellations* 20(2), 188–202.

Bamyeh. M. 2023. The rise and fall of postcolonial charisma. *Arab Studies Quarterly* 45(1), 61–74.

Barrón-López, L. 2020. Why the Black Lives Matter Movement doesn't want a singular leader. *Politico*. www.politico.com/news/2020/07/22/black-lives-matter-movement-leader-377369. Accessed January 31, 2021.

Bayat, A. 2017. *Revolution Without Revolutionaries: Making Sense of the Arab Spring*. Stanford: Stanford University Press.

Bayat, A. 2021. *Revolutionary Life: The Everyday of the Arab Spring*. Cambridge, MA: Harvard University Press.

Benski, T., Langman, L., Perugorría, I., and Tejerina, B. 2013. From the streets and squares to social movement studies: What have we learned? *Current Sociology* 61(4), 541–561.

Berglund, O. and Schmidt, D. 2020. *Extinction Rebellion and Climate Change Activism: Breaking the Law to Change the World*. Cham, CH: Palgrave MacMillan.

Bloom, J. and Martin, Jr, W. E. 2016. *Black against Empire: The History and Politics of the Black Panther Party*. Oakland, CA: University of California Press.

Blumenfeld, J., Bottici, C., and Critchley, S. 2013. *The Anarchist Turn*. London: Pluto Press.

Bookchin, M. 1995. Social anarchism or lifestyle anarchism: An unbridgeable chasm. Oakland: AK Press. https://libcom.org/library/social-anarchism–life style-anarchism-murray-bookchin.

Bookchin, M. and Biehl, J. 1998. *The Politics of Social Ecology: Libertarian Municipalism*. Montreal: Black Rose Books.

Bob, C. 2005. *The Marketing of Rebellion: Insurgents, Media, and International Activism*. Cambridge: Cambridge University Press.

Bob, C. 2012. *The Global Right Wing and the Clash of World Politics*. Cambridge: Cambridge University Press.

Boggs, C. 1977. Marxism, prefigurative communism, and the problem of workers' control. *Radical America* 11(6), 99–122.

Brannigan, J. 2005. Direct action gets the goods. *Organise! Working Class Resistance* 10. https://libcom.org/library/direct-action-gets-goods.

Bray, M. 2013. *Translating Anarchy: The Anarchism of Occupy Wall Street*. London: Zero Books.

Bray, M. 2017. *Antifa: The Anti-Fascist Handbook*. New York: Melville House.

Breines, W. 1989. *Community and Organization in the New Left, 1962-1968: The Great Refusal*. New Brunswick, NJ: Rutgers University Press.

Brown, J. 2020. Party-base linkages and contestatory mobilization in Bolivia's El Alto. *Latin American Perspectives* 47(4), 40–57.

Buchanan, L., Bui, Q., and Patel, J. K. 2020. Black Lives Matter may be the largest movement in US history. *New York Times*, July 3. www.nytimes.com/interactive/2020/07/03/us/george-floyd-protests-crowd-size.html.

Burley, S., ed. 2022. *No Pasarán! Antifascist Dispatches from a World in Crisis.* Chico: AK Press.

Burley, S. 2017. *Fascism Today: What It Is and How to End It.* Oakland: AK Press.

Burridge, D. and Markoff, J. 2023 Social movements and globalization in Latin America. In F. Rossi, ed., *The Oxford Handbook of Latin American Social Movements*. Oxford: Oxford University Press, pp. 249–265.

Callahan, M. 2004. Zapatismo beyond Chiapas. In D. Solnit, ed. *Globalize Liberation: How to Uproot the System and Build a Better World*. San Francisco: City Lights Books, pp. 217–228.

Cappelletti A. 1995. *Anarchism in Latin America*. Translated by Gabriel Palmer-Fernández. Oakland: AK Press.

Case, B. 2022. *Street Rebellion: Resistance Beyond Violence and Nonviolence.* Chico: AK Press.

Case, B. and J. Stribling-Uss. 2023. The revolution will be encrypted: A strategy of leaks and ciphers. *Berkeley Journal of Sociology* 64. https://berkeleyjournal.org/2023/09/21/encrypted-revolution/. Accessed November 23, 2023.

Castañeda, E. 2012. The Indignados of Spain: A precedent to Occupy Wall Street. *Journal of Social, Cultural and Political Protest* 11(3–4), 309–319.

Castells, M. 2012. *Networks of Outrage and Hope: Social Movements in the Internet Age*. Cambridge: Polity Press.

Chandler, J. 2021. Broadcasting from Bolivia, Aymara voices will not be silenced. *NACLA Report on the Americas*, 53(4), 380–386.

Chase-Dunn, C. Aldecoa, J., Breckenridge-Jackson, I., and Herrera, J. S. 2019. Anarchism in the web of transnational social movements. *Journal of World-System Research* 25(2), 373–394.

Chase-Dunn, C. and Almeida, P. 2020. *Global Struggles and Social Change. From Prehistory to World Revolution in the Twenty-First Century*. Baltimore: Johns Hopkins University Press.

Chenoweth, E. and Stephan, M. 2011. *Why Civil Resistance Works*: *The Strategic Logic of Nonviolent Conflict*. New York: Columbia University Press.

Chouhy, G. 2019. Rethinking neoliberalism, rethinking social movements. *Social Movement Studies* 20(4), 426–446.

Chouhy, G. 2022. Explaining the Chile-Uruguay divergence in democratic inclusion: Left parties and the political articulation hypothesis. *Social Science History* 46(2), 401–430. https://doi.org/10.1017/ssh.2021.50.

Clarke, H., Jenson, J., Leduc, L., and Pammett, J. 1995. *Absent Mandate: Canadian Electoral Politics in an Age of Restructuring.* Toronto: Gage.

Collins, P. H. 2019. *Intersectionality as Critical Social Theory.* Durham: Duke University Press.

Cornell, A. 2011. A new anarchism emerges. *Journal for the Study of Radicalism* 5(1), 105–132.

Cornell, A. 2016. *Unruly Equality: U.S. Anarchism in the Twentieth Century.* Los Angeles: University of California Press.

Craib, R. and Maxwell, B. 2015. *No Gods, No Masters, No Peripheries: Global Anarchisms.* Oakland: PM Press.

Creasap, K. 2015. *Sweden Ends Here?: Social Movement Scenes and the Right to the City.* Doctoral dissertation, University of Pittsburgh.

Crenshaw, K. 1989. Demarginalizing the intersection of race and sex: A black feminist critique of antidiscrimination doctrine, feminist theory and antiracist politics. *University of Chicago Legal Forum* 1, 139–167.

CrimethInc. 2012. The 2012 Strike in Québec: Full Report. August 14. https://crimethinc.com/2012/08/14/the-2012-strike-in-quebec-full-report. Accessed February 18, 2023.

CrimethInc. 2018. The Yellow Vest Movement in France: Between "ecological" neoliberalism and "political" movements. November 27. https://crimethinc.com/2018/11/27/the-yellow-vest-movement-in-france-between-ecological-neoliberalism-and-apolitical-movements. Accessed February 18, 2023.

CrimethInc. 2019. Hong Kong: Anarchists in the resistance to the extradition bill. June 22. https://crimethinc.com/2019/06/22/hong-kong-anarchists-in-the-resistance-to-the-extradition-bill-an-interview. Accessed February 18, 2023.

CrimethInc. 2022. Addicted to the tear gas of the Gezi resistance. June 20. https://crimethinc.com/2022/06/20/addicted-to-tear-gas-the-gezi-resistance-june-2013-looking-back-on-a-high-point-of-resistance-in-turkey. Accessed February 18, 2023.

Crow, S. 2014. *Black Flags and Windmills: Hope, Anarchy, and the Common Ground Collective,* 2nd ed. Oakland: PM Press.

Dalton, R. J. 2004. *Democratic Challenges, Democratic Choices. The Erosion of Political Support in Advanced Industrial Democracies.* Oxford: Oxford University Press.

Dangl, B. 2010. *Dancing with Dynamite: States and Social Movements in Latin America.* Oakland, CA: AK Press.

Davenport, C. 2010. *Media Bias, Perspective, and State Repression: The Black Panther Party.* Cambridge: Cambridge University Press.

Davies, J. 1997. "Anarchy in the UK"? Anarchism and popular culture in 1990s' Britain. In J. Purkis and J. Bowen, eds., *Twenty-first Century Anarchism: Unorthodox Ideas for a New Millennium.* London: Cassell Press, pp. 62–82.

della Porta, D. 2022. *Contentious Politics in Emergency Critical Junctures.* Cambridge: Cambridge University Press.

della Porta, D., Andretta, M., Fernandes, T. et al. eds. 2017. *Late Neoliberalism and Its Discontents in the Economic Crisis: Comparing Social Movements in the European Periphery.* Cham, CH: Palgrave Macmillan.

Diamond, L. 2019. *Ill Winds: Saving Democracy from Russian Rage, Chinese Ambition, and American Complacency.* New York: Penguin.

Dixon, C. 2014. *Another Politics: Talking across Today's Transformative Movements.* Oakland: AK Press.

Dupuis-Déri, F. 2014. *Who's Afraid of the Black Blocs? Anarchy in Action around the World.* Oakland, CA: PM Press.

Dupuis-Déri, F. 2019. From the Zapatistas to Seattle: The "New Anarchists". In C. Levy and M. S. Adams, eds. *The Palgrave Handbook of Anarchism.* Cham, CH: Palgrave Macmillan, pp. 471–488.

Elbaum, M. 2018 [2002]. *Revolution in the Air: Sixties Radicals Turn to Lenin, Mao, and Che.* New York: Verso.

Eley, G. 2002. *Forging Democracy: The History of the Left in Europe, 1850-2000.* Oxford: Oxford University Press.

Epstein, B. 1991. *Political Protest and Cultural Revolution: Nonviolent Direct Action in the 1970s and 1980s.* Berkeley, CA: University of California Press.

Epstein, B. 2001. Anarchism and the anti-globalization movement. *Monthly Review* 53(4), 1–14.

Ethnologue. Languages of the World. 2022. www-ethnologue-com.pitt.idm .oclc.org/browse/names. Accessed April 21, 2022.

Federal Bureau of Investigation. 2010. Domestic terrorism: Anarchist extremism: A primer. November 16. https://archives.fbi.gov/archives/news/stories/2010/november/anarchist_111610. Accessed November 23, 2022.

Federación Comunista Libertaria. 2011. Founding of the federación Comunista Libertaria in Chile. Anarkismo.net. January 12, 2011. www.anarkismo.net/article/18487. Accessed February 18, 2023.

Federación Libertaria de Argentina. 2023. Nuestra historia. www.federacionli bertariaargentina.org. Accessed February 18, 2023.

Feixa, C., Perondi, M., Nofre, J. et al. 2012. The #spanishrevolution and beyond. *Cultural Anthropology* [online, August 2012]. www.culanth.org.

Fernandes, Sujatha. 2010. *Who Can Stop the Drums? Urban Social Movements in Chavez's Venezuela*. Durham: Duke University Press.

Filiu, J.-P. 2022. Woman, life, freedom: The origins of Iran's rallying cry. *Le Monde*. October 10. www.lemonde.fr/en/international/article/2022/10/10/woman-life-freedom-the-origins-of-iran-s-rallying-cry_5999763_4.html. Accessed March 6, 2023.

Firth, R. 2020. Mutual aid, anarchist preparedness and COVID-19. In J. Preston and R. Firth, eds., *Coronavirus, Class and Mutual Aid in the United Kingdom*. London: Palgrave Macmillan, pp. 57–111.

Flesher Fominaya, C. 2014. Movement culture as habit(us): Resistance to change in the routinized practice of resistance. In B. Baumgarten, P. Daphi, and P. Ullrich, eds., *Conceptualizing Culture in Social Movement Research*. Cham: Palgrave Macmillan, pp. 186–205.

Flesher Fominaya, C. 2020. *Democracy Reloaded: Inside Spain's Political Laboratory from 15-M to Podemos*. Oxford: Oxford University Press.

Foa, R. S. and Mounk, Y. 2016. The danger of deconsolidation: The democratic disconnect. *Journal of Democracy* 27(3), 5–17.

Foa, R. S., Klassen, A., Wenger, D., Rand, A., and Slade, M. 2020. *Youth and Satisfaction with Democracy: Reversing the Democratic Disconnect?* Cambridge: Centre for the Future of Democracy.

Foran, J., ed. 2003. *The Future of Revolutions: Rethinking Radical Change in the Age of Globalization*. London: Zed Books.

Fórum do Anarquismo Organizado. 2010. Declaration of the aims and principles of the Fórum do Anarquismo Organizado (FAO). https://theanarchistlibrary.org/library/forum-of-organized-anarchism-declaration-of-the-aims-and-principles-of-the-forum-do-anarquismo. Accessed February 18, 2023.

Foster, M. 2003. Globalization gives anarchists a stage. www.washingtonpost.com/archive/politics/2003/01/19/globalization-gives-anarchists-a-stage/bb5933bb-7bbb-4c23-961e-97edb9f2275a/. Accessed January 31, 2022.

Franzosi, R. 1987. The press as a source of socio-historical data: Issues in the methodology of data collection from newspapers. *Historical Methods* 20(1), 5–16.

Fukuyama, F. 1989. The End of History? *National Interest* 16(summer), 3–18.

Fukuyama, F. 1992. *The End of History and the Last Man*. New York: Free Press.

Gallie, W. B. 1956. Essentially contested concepts. *Proceedings of the Aristotelian Society* 105(n.s.), 167–198.

Gelderloos, P. 2022. The invasion of Ukraine: Anarchist interventions and geopolitical changes. March 14. *It's Going Down*. https://itsgoingdown

.org/the-invasion-of-ukraine-anarchist-interventions-and-geopolitical-changes/. Accessed February 19, 2023.

Gibson, D.-M. 2012. *A History of the Nation of Islam: Race, Islam, and the Quest for Freedom.* Santa Barbara: Praeger.

Google N-Grams and pre-modern Chinese. 2015. *Digital Sinology.* https://digitalsinology.org/google-ngrams-pre-modern-chinese/. Accessed November 26, 2019.

Gordon, U. 2009. *Anarchists against the Wall.* Oakland: AK Press.

Gordon, U. 2010. Against the wall: Anarchist mobilization in the Israeli-Palestinian conflict. *Peace & Change* 35(3), 412–433.

Graeber, D. 2002. The new anarchists. *New Left Review* 13(January-February). https://newleftreview.org/issues/II13/articles/david-graeber-the-new-anarchists. Accessed November 11, 2023.

Graeber, D. 2008. *Direct Action: An Ethnography.* Oakland: AK Press.

Graeber, D. 2013. *The Democracy Project: A History, A Crisis, A Movement.* London: Penguin.

Graeber, D. 2014. Why is the world ignoring the revolutionary Kurds in Syria? www.theguardian.com/commentisfree/2014/oct/08/why-world-ignoring-revolutionary-kurds-syria-isis. Accessed October 23, 2021.

Grubačić, A. and Graeber, D. 2004. Anarchism, or the revolutionary movement of the twenty-first century. *Zmag.* https://theanarchistlibrary.org/library/andrej-grubacic-david-graeber-anarchism-or-the-revolutionary-movement-of-the-twenty-first-centu. Accessed February 17, 2023

Grubačić, A. and O'Hearn, D. 2016. *Living at the Edges of Capitalism: Adventures in Exile and Mutual Aid.* Oakland, CA: University of California Press.

Guardian Nigeria. 2020. #EndSARS: We will not allow Anarchy in Nigeria. October 18. https://guardian.ng/news/endsars-we-will-not-allow-anarchy-in-nigeria-fg/. Accessed November 11, 2023.

Haberman, M. and McKinley, J. 2020. Trump moves to cut federal funding from Democratic cities. *New York Times*, September 2. www.nytimes.com/2020/09/02/us/politics/trump-funding-cities.html. Accessed November 11, 2023.

Hammond, J. 2015. The anarchism of Occupy Wall Street. *Science and Society* 79(2), 288–313.

Halvorsen, S. 2012. Beyond the network? Occupy London and the global movement. *Social Movement Studies* 11(3–4), 427–433.

Harrington, M. 2021 [1981]. Marxism and democracy. *Socialist Forum.* https://socialistforum.dsausa.org/issues/fall-2021/marxism-and-democracy/. Accessed April 19, 2023.

Heidemann, K. 2018. Crisis, protest and democratization from below: The rise of a community-based schooling movement in Argentina. In R. Clothey and

K. Heidemann, eds., *Another Way: Decentralization, Democratization and the Global Politics of Community-based Schooling.* Rotterdam: Brill, pp. 31–46.

Howard, N. and Pratt-Boyden, K. 2013. Occupy London as prefigurative political action. *Development in Practice* 23(5–6), 729–741.

Hwang, G. 2021. Examining extremism: U.S. militant anarchists. *Center for Strategic and International Studies.* www.csis.org/blogs/examining-extrem ism/examining-extremism-us-militant-anarchists. Accessed November 23, 2022.

Hylton, F. and Thompson, S. 2007. *Revolutionary Horizons: Past and Present in Bolivian Politics.* Verso: London.

Inglehart, R. F. 2016.The danger of deconsolidation: How much should we worry? *Journal of Democracy* 27(3), 18–23.

Internet Ciudadana. 2021. The inclusion of digital rights in Chile's new constitution. *Agencia Latinoamericana de Información (ALAI).* www.alainet.org/ es/node/214539. Accessed November 11, 2023.

Jackson, I. 2016. How Palestinian protesters helped Black Lives Matter. *USA Today.* July 1. www.usatoday.com/story/opinion/policing/spotlight/ 2016/07/01/how-palestinian-protesters-helped-black-lives-matter/85160266/. Accessed November 11, 2023.

Jaleel, R. 2013. Into the storm: Occupy Sandy and the new sociality of debt. *The Social Text Collective*, October 8. http://what-democracy-looks-like .com/into-the-storm-occupy-sandy-and-the-new-sociality-of-debt/. Accessed November 11, 2023.

Juris, J. 2008. *Networking Futures: The Movements against Corporate Globalization.* Durham, NC: Duke University Press.

Juris, J. 2012. Reflections on #occupy everywhere: Social media, public space, and emerging logics of aggregation. *American Ethnologist* 39(2), 259–279.

Karyotis, G. and Rüdig, W. 2013. Beyond the usual suspects? New participants in anti-austerity protests in Greece. *Mobilization* 18(3), 313–330.

Katsiaficas, G. 2006. *Subversion of Politics: European Autonomous Social Movements and the Decolonization of Everyday Life.* Oakland: AK Press.

Kelly, K. 2020. Anarchy: What it is and why pop culture loves it. *Teen Vogue.* June 3. www.teenvogue.com/story/anarchy-explained-what-it-is-why-pop-culture-loves-it. Accessed January 31, 2022.

Kerl, E. 2010. Contemporary anarchism. *International Socialist Review.* https:// isreview.org/issue/72/contemporary-anarchism. Accessed January 24, 2021.

King, M. 2020. Black Lives Matter power grab sets off internal revolt. *Politico.* www.politico.com/news/2020/12/10/black-lives-matter-organization-biden-444097). Accessed January 31, 2021.

Kingsnorth, P. 2003. *One No, Many Yeses*. London: The Free Press.

Kinna, R. 2009. *Anarchism: A Beginner's Guide*, 2nd ed. Oxford: Oneworld Publications.

Kinna, R. 2020. *The Government of No One: The Theory and Practice of Anarchism*. Oakland: AK Press.

Klein, H. 2015. *Compañeras: Zapatista Women's Stories*. New York: Seven Stories Press.

Knapp, M., Ayboğa, E., and Flach, A. 2016. *Revolution in Rojava: Democratic Autonomy and Women's Liberation in the Syrian Kurdistan*. Oakland: PM Press.

Konieczny, P. 2009. Governance, organization, and democracy on the internet: The iron law and the evolution of Wikipedia. *Sociological Forum* 24(1), 162–192.

Konieczny, P. 2017. Wikipedia in the anti-SOPA protests as a case study of direct, deliberative democracy in cyberspace. *Information, Communication & Society* 20(2), 167–184.

Krastev, I. and Holmes, S. 2019. *The Light that Failed: Why the West is Losing the Fight for Democracy*. London: Pegasus Books.

Kropotkin, P. 1892. Revolutionary government. https://theanarchistlibrary.org/library/petr-kropotkin-revolutionary-government. Accessed March 1, 2023.

Kropotkin, P. 2005 [1902]. *Mutual Aid: A Factor of Evolution*. Cambridge, MA: Peacework.

LaFrance, A. 2023. The New Anarchy: American faces a type of extremist violence it does not know how to stop. *The Atlantic* April, 22–37.

Langman, L. 2013. Occupy: A new social movement. *Current Sociology* 61(4), 510.

Lazar, H. 2018. Intersections. In B. Franks, N. Jun, and L. Williams, eds., *Anarchism: A Conceptual Approach*. New York: Routledge, pp. 157–176.

Lazar, H. 2023. Collective care and mutual aid as community self-defense. In C. Coquard, ed., *Kropotkin Now! Life, Freedom & Ethics*. Montreal: Black Rose Books, pp. 93–105.

Leverink, J. 2015. Murray Bookchin and the Kurdish resistance. *Roar Magazine*. https://roarmag.org/essays/bookchin-kurdish-struggle-ocalan-rojava/.

Lipset, S. M. and Schneider, W. 1983. *The Confidence Gap*. Baltimore: Johns Hopkins University Press.

Loadenthal, M. 2020. Now that was a riot!: Social control in felonious times. *Global Society* 34(1), 120–144.

Maeckelbergh, M. 2011. Doing is believing: Prefiguration as strategic practice in the alterglobalization movement. *Social Movement Studies* 10(1), 1–20.

Maeckelbergh, M. 2012. Horizontal democracy now: From alterglobalization to occupation. *Interface: A Journal for and about Social Movements* 4(1), 207–234.

Mahdawi, A. 2020. Black Lives Matter's Alicia Garza: Leadership today doesn't look like Martin Luther King. *The Guardian*. October 17. www.theguardian .com/world/2020/oct/17/black-lives-matter-alicia-garza-leadership-today-doesnt-look-like-martin-luther-king. Accessed January 31, 2021.

Malsin, J. 2013. Ultras, Anarchists, and street fighting in Egypt. *Vice*. January 26. www.vice.com/read/ultras-anarchists-and-street-fighting-in-egypt. Accessed March 17, 2023.

Maltz, J. 2023. Why Netanyahu Slurs Israel's pro-democracy protesters as "Anarchists." *Haaretz*. March 10. www.haaretz.com/israel-news/2023-03-10/ty-article-magazine/.premium/why-netanyahu-slurs-israels-pro-democracy-protesters-as-anarchists/00000186-c637-d069-a3df-c63ffad90000. Accessed March 11, 2023.

Manski, B., Lazar H., and Moodliar, S. 2020. The millennial turns and the new period: An introduction. *Socialism and Democracy* 34(1), 1–50.

Manski, B. and Smith, J. 2019. Introduction: The dynamics and terrains of local democracy and corporate power in the 21st century. *Journal of World-System Research* 25(1), 6–14. https://jwsr.pitt.edu/ojs/jwsr/article/view/919/1270.

Markoff, J. 2001. The Internet and electronic communications. In M. K. Cayton and P. W. Williams, eds., *Encyclopedia of American Cultural and Intellectual History*. New York: Charles Scribner's Sons, pp. 387–395. http://pitt.idm .oclc.org/login?url=https://search.credoreference.com/content/entry/galea cih/the_internet_and_electronic_communications/0?institutionId=1425.

Markoff, J. 2011. A moving target: Democracy. *Archives Européennes de Sociologie/European Journal of Sociology* 52(2), 239–276.

Markoff, J. 2015. *Waves of Democracy. Social Movements and Political Change*. 2nd ed. Boulder, CO: Paradigm Publishers.

Markoff, J. 2019. Overflowing channels: How democracy didn't work as planned (and perhaps a good thing it didn't). *Sociological Theory* 37(2), 184–208.

Markoff, J., Lazar, H., and Smith, J. 2021. Creative disappointment: How movements for democracy spawn movements for even more democracy. *Research in Political Sociology* 28, 237–262.

Marshall, P. 2009. *Demanding the Impossible: A History of Anarchism*. Oakland: PM Press.

Martínez, E. and García, A. 2004. Zapatismo – what is Zapatismo? A brief definition for activists. In D. Solnit, ed., *Globalize Liberation: How to Uproot the System and Build a Better World*. San Francisco: City Lights Books, pp. 213–216.

Marx, K. and Engels, F. 1848. *Manifesto of the Communist Party.* www .marxists.org/archive/marx/works/1848/communist-manifesto/.

Mbah, S. and Igariwey, I. E. 1997. *African Anarchism: The History of a Movement.* Tucson: See Sharp Press.

Meyer, D. and Staggenborg, S. 1996. Movements, countermovements, and the structure of political opportunity. *American Journal of Sociology* 101(6), 1628–1660.

Meyer, J. M., Krücken, G., and Drori, G. 2009. *World Society: The Writings of John W. Meyer.* Oxford: Oxford University Press.

Michel, J.-B., Shen, Y. K., Aiden, A. P., et al. 2011. Quantitative analysis of culture using millions of digitized books. *Science* 331(6014), 176–182.

Michels, R. 1962 [1911]. *Political Parties: A Sociological Study of the Oligarchical Tendencies of Modern Democracy.* New York: Free Press.

Milkman, R. 2017. A new political generation: Millennials and the post-2008 wave of protest. *American Sociological Review* 82(1), 1–31.

Milkman, R., Bamyeh, M., Wilson, W. J., Williams, D., and Gould, D. 2012. Understanding "Occupy". *Contexts* 11(2), 12–21.

Milstein, C., ed. 2020. Collective care is our best weapon against COVID and other disasters. https://mutualaiddisasterrelief.org/collective-care/. Accessed November 11, 2023.

Mishra, P. 2019. From Chile to India a global anarchy revival. *Business Standard.* December 19, 2019. www.business-standard.com/article/current-affairs/from-chile-to-india-a-global-anarchy-revival-could-outdo-the-1960s-119121900268_1.html. Accessed November 11, 2023.

Mitchell, M. 2022. Building resilient organizations: Toward joy and durable power in a time of crisis. *Convergence.* https://convergencemag.com/articles/building-resilient-organizations-toward-joy-and-durable-power-in-a-time-of-crisis/. Accessed November 11, 2023.

Mounk, Y. 2018. *The People vs. Democracy: Why Our Freedom Is in Danger and How to Save It.* Cambridge, MA: Harvard University Press.

Mudge, S. 2018. *Leftism Reinvented: Western Parties from Socialism to Neoliberalism.* Cambridge, MA: Harvard University Press.

Norris, P., ed. 1999. *Critical Citizens: Global Support for Democratic Governance.* Oxford: Oxford University Press.

Norris, P. 2011. *Democratic Deficit: Critical Citizens Revisited.* Cambridge: Cambridge University Press.

Norris, P. and Inglehart, R. 2019. *Cultural Backlash: Trump, Brexit, and Authoritarian Populism.* Cambridge: Cambridge University Press.

Northrup, D. 2013. *How English Became the Global Language.* New York: Palgrave Macmillan.

Nunberg, G. 2010. Humanities research with the Google Books Corpus. *Language Log*. https://languagelog.ldc.upenn.edu/nll/?p=2847. Accessed November 26, 2019.

Nye, J., Jr, Zelikow, P., and King, D. 1997. *Why People Don't Trust Government*. Cambridge: Cambridge University Press.

Oikonomakis, L. and Espinoza, F. 2014. Bolivia: MAS and the movements that brought it to state power. In R. Stahler-Sholk, H. Vanden, and M. Beeker eds., *Rethinking Latin American Social Movements: Radical Action from Below*. Lanham, MD: Rowman and Littlefield, pp. 285–307.

Olivera, O. and Lewis, T. 2004. *Cochabamba!: Water War in Bolivia*. Cambridge, MA: South End Press.

Ortiz, I., Burke, S., Berrada, M., and Cortés, H. S. 2021. *World Protests: A Study of Key Protest Issues in the 21st Century*. Cham, CH: Palgrave Macmillan.

Pechenick, E. A., Danforth, C. M., and Dodds, P. S. 2015. Characterizing the Google Books Corpus: Strong limits to inferences of socio-cultural and linguistic evolution. *PLoS ONE* 10(10). https://journals.plos.org/plosone/art icle?id=10.1371/journal.pone.0137041. Accessed November 26, 2019.

Pew Research Center. 2021. Public trust in government: 1958–2020. May 17. www.pewresearch.org/politics/2021/05/17/public-trust-in-government-1958-2021/. Accessed January 31, 2022.

Pharr, S. J. and Putnam, R. eds. 2000. *Disaffected Democracies. What's Troubling the Trilateral Countries?* Princeton: Princeton University Press.

Piketty, T. 2017. *Capital in the Twenty-First* Century. Cambridge, MA: Harvard University Press.

Polletta, F. 2004. *Freedom Is an Endless Meeting: Democracy in American Social Movements*. Chicago: University of Chicago Press.

Potiker, S. L. 2019. Obstacles to insurrection: Militarized border crossing hindering the Rojava liberation struggle. *Anarchist Studies* 27(2), 1–19.

Potiker, S. L., Williams, D., and Alimahomed-Wilson, J. (2022). Anarchist and anarchistic anti-systemic movements in world-systems perspective: A qualitative comparative analysis of non-state spaces. *Journal of World-Systems Research* 28(2), 188–218.

Prokosch, M. and Raymond, L., eds. 2002. *The Global Activist's Manual: Local Ways to Change the World*. New York: Thunder's Mountain Press.

ProQuest *Historical Newspapers. The New York Times with Index. 1851–2015.* https://search-proquest-com.pitt.idm.oclc.org/hnpnewyorktimes/advanced?accountid=14709. Accessed October 6, 2019.

ProQuest *Historical Newspapers. The Times of India.* 1870–2010. https://search-proquest-com.pitt.idm.oclc.org/publication/54644/citation/8D51D44CBF7048EDPQ/2?accountid=14709. Accessed September 27, 2019.

Przeworski, A. 2010. *Democracy and the Limits of Self-Government.* Cambridge: Cambridge University Press.

Przeworski, A. 2019. *Crises of Democracy.* Cambridge: Cambridge University Press.

Przeworski, A., Alvarez, M. E., Cheibub, J. A., and Limongi, F. 2000. *Democracy and Development. Political Institutions and Well-Being in the World, 1950–1990.* New York: Cambridge University Press.

Przeworski, A. and Sprague, J. 1986. *Paper Stones: A History of Electoral Socialism.* Chicago: University of Chicago Press.

Putnam, R. D. 2020. *The Upswing. How America Came Together a Century Ago and How We Can Do It Again.* New York: Simon & Schuster.

Ramnath, M. 2019. Non-Western Anarchisms and Postcolonialism. In C. Levy and M. S. Adams, eds., *The Palgrave Handbook of Anarchism.* Palgrave Macmillan, pp. 677–695.

Reitan, R. 2007. *Global Activism.* London: Routledge Press.

Repucci, S. 2020. Freedom in the world 2020: A leaderless struggle for democracy. https://freedomhouse.org/report/freedom-world/2020/leaderless-struggle-democracy. Accessed November 11, 2023.

Rivera Cusicanqui, S. 2015. *Mito y desarrollo en Bolivia: El giro colonial del gobierno del MAS.* La Paz, Bolivia: Plural Editores.

Roberts, S. 2020. David Graeber, caustic critic of inequality, is dead at 59. *New York Times*, September, 9. www.nytimes.com/2020/09/04/books/david-graeber-dead.html.

Robinson, W. I. 2008. *Latin America and Global Capitalism: A Critical Globalization Perspective.* Baltimore: The John Hopkins University Press.

Romanos, E. 2016. De Tahrir a Wall Street por la Puerta del Sol: La difusión transnacional de los movimientos sociales en perspectiva comparada. *Revista Española de Investigaciones Sociológicas 154*, 103–118.

Rossi, F. 2017. *The Poor's Struggle for Political Participation: The Piquetero Movement in Argentina.* Cambridge: Cambridge University Press.

Sánchez, M. and Osorio Mercado, H. 2020. Abril 2018, Nicaragua: El desafío de la democracia frente al autoritarismo. In UCA Editores. *Nicaragua 2018: La insurrección cívica de abril.* Managua: UCA Publicaciones, Universidad Centroamericana.

Sassoon, D. 1996. *One Hundred Years of Socialism: The West European Left in the Twentieth Century.* New York: The New Press.

Schneider, N. 2013. *Thank You, Anarchy: Notes from the Occupy Apocalypse.* Oakland, CA: University of California Press.

Schneirov, M. and Schneirov, R. 2016. Capitalism as a social movement: The corporate and neoliberal reconstruction of the American political economy in the twentieth century. *Social Movement Studies* 15(6), 561–576.

Scott, J. C. 2009. *The Art of Not Being Governed: An Anarchist History of Upland Southeast Asia.* New Haven, CT: Yale University Press.

Schroering, C. 2021. *The Global Economy, Resource Conflicts, and Transnational Social Movements: Dimensions of Resistance to Water Privatization.* Doctoral dissertation. University of Pittsburgh.

Shaffner, K. 2019. *Anarchist Cuba: Countercultural Politics in the Early Twentieth Century.* Oakland: PM Press.

Shantz, J. 2010. Understanding anarchy: Contemporary anarchism and social movement theory. *Resistance Studies* 3(1), 42–56.

Shefner, J. and Blad, C. 2020. *Why Austerity Persists.* Cambridge, MA: Polity Press.

Should We Allow Google NGrams to be Presented as Statistical Evidence without Qualification? Should We Define a Set of Standards for their Usage? 2012. *English Language and Usage: Meta.* https://english.meta .stackexchange.com/questions/2469/should-we-allow-google-ngrams-to-be-presented-as-statistical-evidence-without-qu. Accessed November 11, 2023

Sitrin, M. 2012. Horizontalism and the Occupy Movements. *Dissent* 59(2), 74–75.

Sitrin, M. 2014a. Postcards from a horizontal world. *OpenDemocracy.* www .resilience.org/stories/2014-01-13/postcards-from-a-horizontal-world/. Accessed January 28, 2022.

Sitrin, M. 2014b. Argentina: Against and beyond the state. In R. Stahler-Sholk, H. I. Vanden, and M. Becker, eds., *Rethinking Latin American Social Movements: Radical Action from Below.* Lanham, MD: Rowman and Littlefield, 209–232.

Sitrin, M. 2020. DNA in movement: Reflections on a new form of movements. *Socialism and Democracy* 34(1), 166–179.

Sitrin, M. and Colectiva Sembrar 2020. *Pandemic Solidarity: Mutual Aid During the COVID-19 Crisis.* London: Pluto Press.

Sklair, L. 2011. Social movements for global capitalism: The transnational capitalist class in action. *Review of International Political Economy* 4(3), 514–538.

Skoczylas, M. 2016. *Anarchism and Prefigurative Politics in the Occupy Movement: A Study of Occupied Space, Horizontal Structure, and Anarchist Theory in Practice.* Doctoral dissertation, University of Pittsburgh

Smith, J. 2008. *Social Movements for Global Democracy.* Baltimore: Johns Hopkins.

Smith, J., Goodhart, M., Manning, P., and Markoff, J., eds. 2017. *Social Movements and World-System Transformation*. New York: Routledge.

Smith, J. and Wiest, D. 2012. *Social Movements in the World-System: The Politics of Crisis and Transformation*. New York: Russell Sage Foundation.

Solnit, D., ed. 2004. *Globalize Liberation: How to Uproot the System and Build a Better World*. San Francisco: City Lights Books.

Solnit, D. 2010. *A Paradise Build in Hell: The Extraordinary Communities that Arise in Disaster*. New York: Penguin Books.

Spade, D. 2020a. Solidarity not charity: Mutual aid for mobilization and survival. *Social Text* 38(1), 131–151.

Spade, D. 2020b. *Mutual Aid: Building Solidarity During This Crisis (and the Next)*. New York: Verso.

Spalding, R. 2014. El Salvador: Horizontalism and the anti-mining movement. In R. Stahler-Sholk, H. Vanden, and M. Becker, eds., *Rethinking Latin American Social Movements: Radical Action from Below*. Lanham, MD: Rowman and Littlefield, pp. 311–330.

Sperber, E. 2018. The emergency brake. *Counterpunch*. October 9. www .counterpunch.org/2018/10/09/the-emergency-brake/. Accessed June 20, 2021.

Stahler-Sholk, R., Vanden, H., and Becker, M., eds. 2014. *Rethinking Latin American Social Movements: Radical Action from Below*. Lanham, MD: Rowman and Littlefield.

Staggenborg, S. 2002. The "Meso" in social movement research. In D. Meyer, N. Whittier, and B. Robnett, eds., *Social Movements: Identity, Culture, and the State*. Oxford: Oxford University Press, pp. 124–139.

Strangers in a Tangled Wilderness, eds. 2015. *A Small Key Can Open a Large Door: The Rojava Revolution*. Oakland: AK Press.

Sunshine, S. 2013. *Post-1960 U.S. Anarchism and Social Theory*. New York: CUNY Graduate Center. Unpublished dissertation.

Swann, J. 2017. How democratic socialists are building on Bernie's momentum. *Rolling Stone*. www.rollingstone.com/politics/politics-features/how-democratic-socialists-are-building-on-bernies-momentum-120080/. Accessed January 29, 2021.

Taller Libertario Alfredo López. 2021. Cuban Anarchists on the Protests of July 11. *CrimethInc*. https://crimethinc.com/2021/07/22/cuban-anarchists-on-the-protests-of-july-11#cuba-the-end-of-the-social-spell-of-the-revolution.

Tejerina, B., Benski, T., Langman, L., and Perugorría, I. 2013. Special Issue: From indignation to occupation: A new wave of global mobilization. *Current Sociology* 61(4), 377–392.

Thompson, A. K. 2010. *Black Bloc, White Riot: Anti-Globalization and the Genealogy of Dissent*. Oakland, CA: AK Press.

Thwaites Rey, M. 2011. La autonomía: Entre el mito y la potencia emancipadora. In E. Adamovsky, C. Albertani, B. Arditi et al. eds., *Pensar Las Autonomías*. Mexico, DF: Bajo Tierra Ediciones, pp. 143–207.

Times of London Digital Archive. 1870–2014. https://go-gale-com.pitt.idm .oclc.org/ps/dispAdvSearch.do?userGroupName=uptt_main&prodid= TTDA. Accessed October 6, 2020.

Uzcategui, R. 2017. Cuba and the demonization of anarchists: A lesson for our times. *Black Rose*. https://blackrosefed.org/cuba-demonization-of-anarchists/. Accessed November 12, 2023.

van de Sande, M. 2013. The prefigurative politics of Tahrir Square: An alternative perspective on the 2011 revolutions. *Res Publica* 19(3), 223–239.

Villanueva, P. 2018. From Rojava to the Mapuche struggle. The Kurdish revolutionary seed spreads in Latin America. https://theanarchistlibrary .org/library/pilar-villanueva-from-rojava-to-the-mapuche-struggle. Accessed October 23, 2021.

Vortex Group, ed. 2023. *The George Floyd Uprising*. Oakland: PM Press.

Walby, S. 2015. *Crisis*. Cambridge: Polity Press.

Walker, T. W., and Wade, C. 2016. *Nicaragua: Emerging from the Shadow of the Eagle*. Boulder: Westview Press.

Wallerstein, I. 2004. *World-Systems Analysis: An Introduction*. Durham, NC: Duke University Press.

Ward, C. 1996. *Anarchy in Action*. London: Freedom Press.

Weber, M. 1968. *Economy and Society: An Outline of Interpretive Sociology*, G. Roth and C. Wittich, eds., New York: Bedminister Press.

Wigger, A. 2014. A critical appraisal of what could be an anarchist political economy. *Ephemera Journal* 14(4), 739–751.

Williams, D. 2012. The anarchist DNA of occupy. *Contexts* 11(2), 19–20. www .academia.edu/1640056/The_Anarchist_DNA_of_Occupy.

Williams, D. 2015. Black Panther radical factionalization and the development of black anarchism. *Journal of Black Studies*, 46(7), 678–703.

Williams, D. 2017. *Black Flags and Social Movements: A Sociological Analysis of Movement Anarchism*. Manchester: Manchester University Press.

Williams, D. 2018. Contemporary anarchist and anarchistic movements. *Sociology Compass* 12(6), 1–17.

Williams, D. and Lee, M. 2008. "We are everywhere": An ecological analysis of organizations in the Anarchist Yellow Pages. *Humanity and Society* 2008 (32), 45–70.

Williams, D. and Lee, M. 2012. Aiming to overthrow the state (without using the state): Political opportunities for anarchist movements. *The Anarchist Library*. https://theanarchistlibrary.org/library/dana-m-williams-and-mat thew-t-lee-aiming-to-overthrow-the-state-without-using-the-state. Accessed November 30, 2022.

Wittgenstein, L. 2009. *Philosophical Investigations*. 4th ed. Chichester: Blackwell.

Wood, L. 2012. *Direct Action, Deliberation, and Diffusion: Collective Action after the WTO Protests in Seattle*. Cambridge: Cambridge University Press.

Wood, L. 2020. The Seattle model. *Socialism and Democracy* 34(1), 51–65.

Wordsworth, A. 2022. Ukrainian lessons at the train station. *New York Review of Books*. December 8. www.nybooks.com/articles/2022/12/08/ukrainian-les sons-at-the-train-station-ada-wordsworth. Accessed November 12, 2023.

Wright, E. O. 2010. *Envisioning Real Utopias*. London: Verso.

Yates, L. 2015. Rethinking prefiguration: Alternatives, micropolitics and goals in social movements. *Social Movement Studies* 14(1), 1–21.

Yee, V. 2021. Tunisians recall revolution reluctantly, if at all: "it just faded away". www.nytimes.com/2021/10/17/world/middleeast/tunisia-revolution-memoro-monuments.html. Accessed October 23, 2021.

Younes, N. and Reips, U.-D. 2019. Guideline for improving the reliability of Google Ngram studies: Evidence from religious terms. *PLOS ONE* 14(3). https://journals.plos.org/plosone/article?id=10.1371/journal.pone.0213554. Accessed November 12, 2023.

Zhang, S. 2015. The pitfalls of using Google Ngram to study language. *Wired*. www.wired.com/2015/10/pitfalls-of-studying-language-with-google-ngram/. Accessed November 26, 2019.

Zibechi, R. 2010. *Dispersing Power: Social Movements as Anti-State Forces*. Oakland, CA: AK Press.

Acknowledgments

Parts of the argument were presented at the conference Democracy in Europe, Democracy Beyond Europe at the University of Pittsburgh, January 2023, and we thank attendees for their responses. For extremely valuable comments on an earlier version, we thank Mohammed Bamyeh, the reviewers, and the series editors. This is a collective work; we present authors' names in reverse alphabetical order.

Cambridge Elements ≡

Contentious Politics

David S. Meyer

University of California, Irvine

David S. Meyer is Professor of Sociology and Political Science at the University of California, Irvine. He has written extensively on social movements and public policy, mostly in the United States, and is a winner of the John D. McCarthy Award for Lifetime Achievement in the Scholarship of Social Movements and Collective Behavior.

Suzanne Staggenborg

University of Pittsburgh

Suzanne Staggenborg is Professor of Sociology at the University of Pittsburgh. She has studied organizational and political dynamics in a variety of social movements, including the women's movement and the environmental movement, and is a winner of the John D. McCarthy Award for Lifetime Achievement in the Scholarship of Social Movements and Collective Behavior.

About the Series

Cambridge Elements series in Contentious Politics provides an important opportunity to bridge research and communication about the politics of protest across disciplines and between the academy and a broader public. Our focus is on political engagement, disruption, and collective action that extends beyond the boundaries of conventional institutional politics. Social movements, revolutionary campaigns, organized reform efforts, and more or less spontaneous uprisings are the important and interesting developments that animate contemporary politics; we welcome studies and analyses that promote better understanding and dialogue.

Cambridge Elements ⁼

Contentious Politics

Printed in the United States
by Baker & Taylor Publisher Services